The Uncontrollability of the World

The Uncontrollability
of the World

Hartmut Rosa

Translated by James C. Wagner

polity

Originally published in German as *Unverfügbarkeit* © 2018 Residenz Verlag GmbH. Salzburg- Wien.

This English edition © 2020 by Polity Press

Polity Press
65 Bridge Street
Cambridge CB2 1UR, UK

Polity Press
101 Station Landing
Suite 300
Medford, MA 02155, USA

ISBN-13: 978-1-5095-4315-1
ISBN-13: 978-1-5095-4316-8 (paperback)

A catalogue record for this book is available from the British Library.

Typeset in 11 on 14 pt Sabon by
Servis Filmsetting Ltd, Stockport, Cheshire
Printed and bound in Great Britain by TJ International Limited

The publisher has used its best endeavours to ensure that the URLs for external websites referred to in this book are correct and active at the time of going to press. However, the publisher has no responsibility for the websites and can make no guarantee that a site will remain live or that the content is or will remain appropriate.

Every effort has been made to trace all copyright holders, but if any have been overlooked the publisher will be pleased to include any necessary credits in any subsequent reprint or edition.

For further information on Polity, visit our website:
politybooks.com

Contents

v

Contents

Beyond Control

A Note from the Author on the Key Term of This Book

No doubt the title of this book presents a challenge, certainly for all languages other than German. *Unverfügbarkeit*: what does it mean? It is a term that is well established in German, although it is not very widespread. For me, *Unverfügbarkeit* is one of the key elements of every experience of being in resonance with someone or something. Ever since I first used it in an article in German, I have been wondering about how to translate it into English. My first attempt was "elusiveness." With this I wanted to point to the fact that resonance—one of my key theoretical concepts—is something comparable to the moment of falling asleep: we cannot bring it about simply by willing it. The more we want it, the less we get it, at least sometimes. There is something about resonance that evades our grasp. But I ultimately decided against this term, because resonance is not always elusive. It is not a chimera. Sometimes we have strong experiences of true connection and encounter that are not elusive. So I tried "unavailability." But I never liked this one. "We are sorry, this service is temporarily unavailable." Ever since I heard this on my phone, I was convinced that this is not what I mean by *Unverfügbarkeit*. So I turned to "unpredictability." I still like this one, because experiences of resonance are unpredictable in two ways. First, you can try to create a context that makes it likely that you will be deeply touched and transformed by something or someone, and that you will be capable of reaching out and responding to this touch. We buy expensive tickets to a concert, for example, or we arrange a beautiful candle-light dinner with our beloved—but, in both cases, the evening might still turn out to be deeply frustrating and alienating, whereas on other occasions, when we do not expect anything, all of a sudden we experience strong resonance with something or someone. Hence, when or where resonance will happen is unpredictable. More than this, if you enter into resonance with someone or something, it is impossible to predict what this process of being touched and transformed will mean for you or will do to you.

But *Unverfügbarkeit* actually goes deeper than this. It is not just about non-predictability, but about *non-engineerability*. This term was suggested to me when I gave a lecture at the London School of Economics; and it became my favorite for a long time. There is no way to "fabricate" resonance, to instrumentally bring it about. Similarly, we cannot easily "engineer" falling asleep, or the falling of snow—although nowadays we actually *can* take sleeping pills, just as winter resorts *can* employ snow cannons. This is exactly what this book is about: modernity's incessant desire to make the world engin-eerable, predictable, available, accessible, disposable (i.e. *verfügbar*) in all its aspects. And it is about the twin paradox that, first, this very desire alters our relationship to the world. Snow shooting out of a snow cannon does not have the experiential quality of a real snowfall. A fully engineerable world eventually would be a "dead world." Second, this desire for control produces, behind our backs, a world that in the end is utterly uncontrollable in all the relevant aspects. We cannot control our late modern world in any way: politically, economically, legally, technologically, or individually. The drive and desire toward controllability ultimately creates monstrous, frightening forms of uncontrollability. *Uncontrollability*: This is the term that Jim, the masterful translator of this book, found to capture all the aspects of *Unverfügbarkeit* discussed here. And, even if it is not exactly equivalent to *Unverfügbarkeit* in every nuance, it surely is the closest we can get. And Jim, who also translated my big book on *Resonance*, was sensitive enough in his translation to capture all those nuances in the text itself. For this, I am infinitely grateful to him!

Hartmut Rosa, March 2020

Introduction

On Snow

Do you still remember the first snowfall on a late autumn or winter day, when you were a child? It was like the intrusion of a new reality. Something shy and strange that had come to visit us, falling down upon and transforming the world around us, without our having to do anything. An unexpected gift. Falling snow is perhaps the purest manifestation of uncontrollability. We cannot manufacture it, force it, or even confidently predict it, at least not very far in advance. What is more, we cannot get hold of it or make it our own. Take some in your hand, it slips through your fingers. Bring it into the house, it melts away. Pack it away in the freezer, it stops being snow and becomes ice. Maybe that is why so many people—not only children—long for it, especially around the holidays. Meteorologists are assailed and beseeched for weeks beforehand. Will it be a white Christmas this year? What are the chances? And of course there is no shortage of efforts to bring snow under our control. Winter resorts advertise "guaranteed snow," making good on their promises with the aid of machines: these produce artificial snow that holds up even at temperatures above 15° Celsius.

Our relationship to snow reflects the drama of our relationship to the modern world as in a crystal ball. The driving cultural force of that form of life we call "modern" is the idea, the hope and desire, that we can make the world *controllable*. Yet it is only in encountering the *uncontrollable* that we really experience the world. Only then do we feel touched, moved, alive. A world that is fully known, in which everything has been planned and mastered, would be a dead world. This is no metaphysical insight, but an everyday experience. Our lives unfold as the interplay between what we can control and that which remains outside our control, yet "concerns us" in some way. Life happens, as it were, on the borderline. Take a mass phenomenon like soccer. Why do people flock to the stadium? "Because," as the manager of the 1954 German national team Sepp Herberger once quipped, "they don't know how it will turn out." Contrary to the constant complaint that soccer these days is "only about the money," what makes the game attractive is the fact that victories and defeats cannot be bought or engineered. They cannot be controlled. Soccer remains so exciting for many people —to the point that it constitutes the central focus of their libidinal desire all week long, until the next round of league play begins—precisely because it is inherently uncontrollable. Not *entirely* uncontrollable, of course. Money and training obviously can have an influence on what happens in the game, as every amateur athlete knows—and not just in soccer but also in tennis, basketball, and every other sport. You can improve your chances on the tennis court through good preparation, mental discipline, and relaxation, true, but you can never engineer a victory, or even the next point. Even more: you cannot achieve anything through increased effort alone. The more you try to bring the goal or the next point under your control, the more you try to force it, the less you succeed. That is why so many amateur athletes perform all manner of obscure, would-be magic rituals before the match or their next serve: to try to control the uncontrollable. It is the tension and the struggle along this boundary line that keeps sport so fascinating.[1]

The interplay between control and uncontrollability is constitutive not only of many varieties of sports, but of games in general—card games as well as chess, board games as well as games of chance—although the relation between what is controllable and what is uncontrollable can vary greatly. It may be easy to predict with confidence the winner and loser in a chess match, less so in parcheesi or in games of chance. This is the case not only with games, either. Our encounter with the uncontrollable and our desire or struggle to bring it under control form a red thread that runs through all areas of our lives. Take sleep: the more we want to fall asleep, the less able we are to force ourselves to do so. And yet there are things we can do to make sleep come easier—taking a walk, for example, or developing a regular bedtime routine. Or take love. "Hold the line," the band Toto aptly sings: "Love isn't always on time." Or our health. Sure, we can try to reduce our risk of catching a cold. We can eat healthier. But whether or not we fall ill, or get cancer, or suffer a herniated disc—these are among the uncontrollable (or should we say only semicontrollable?) aspects of life. From games to love, from snow to death, human life and human experience are defined by uncontrollability. And if we think about modernity's relationship to the world, that is, how the institutions and cultural practices of contemporary society relate to the world and how we, as modern subjects, find ourselves situated in the world as a result, then the ways in which we relate to uncontrollability—individually, culturally, institutionally, and structurally—would seem to offer a cardinal focal point for analysis. In the following pages I want to try to systematically apply this focus to the everyday practices and social conflicts of contemporary late modern society in order to see what can be learned from this perspective. My hypothesis is this: because we, as late modern human beings, aim to make the world controllable at every level—individual, cultural, institutional, and structural—we invariably encounter the world as a "point of aggressions" or as a series of points of aggression, in other words as a series of objects that we have to know, attain, conquer, master, or exploit. And precisely because of this, "life," the experience of feeling alive and of truly encountering the world—that which makes *resonance* possible— always seems to elude us. This in turn leads to anxiety, frustration, anger, and even despair, which then manifest themselves, among other things, in acts of impotent political aggression.

I

The World as a Point of Aggression

The starting point for my reflections is the insight that human beings are always already situated in a world, always already *au monde*, as the French phenomenologist Maurice Merleau-Ponty puts it. The first glimmer of awareness when we open our eyes in the morning or awake from anesthesia, and presumably even the first conscious impression of a newborn, is the perception that "there is something," that *something is present*.[1] We can understand this presence as the ur-form of what we gradually come to experience, explore, and conceive of as world, although it essentially precedes the distinction between subject and world. From this original impression that "something is present," I have sought to develop a sociology of our relationship to the world that assumes that subject and world are not the precondition, but the result of our relatedness to this presence. Little by little, in the course of our development, we learn from this "something" to distinguish between ourselves as experiencing subjects and the world as that which we encounter. The way in which the two are related is constitutive of both what we are as human beings and what we encounter as world. Hence, whenever I refer in what follows to (experiencing) subjects and (encountered) objects, these are to be understood as the two poles—the "self pole" and "world pole," so to speak—of the relationship that constitutes them.

The fundamental question of a sociology of our relationship to the world is, *how is this something that is present constituted?* Is it benevolent and redemptive, promising and seductive, cold and indifferent, or even threatening and dangerous? In contrast to philosophers, psychologists, and even theologians, who all grapple professionally with the question of the human being's place in the cosmos or our relationship to the universe, to nature, and so on,[2] I start from the assumption that the way we are related to the world is not determined simply by the fact of our being human, but rather depends on the social and cultural conditions into which we have been socialized. We learn and become habituated to a certain practical attitude toward the world that goes far beyond our cognitive "worldview," our conscious assumptions and convictions about what exists in the world and what the world is all about, what it all comes down to. The first guiding thesis that I would like to develop in this essay is that, for late modern human beings, the world has simply become a point of aggression.[3] Everything that appears to us must be known, mastered, conquered, made useful. Expressed abstractly, this sounds banal at first—but it isn't. Lurking behind this idea is a creeping reorganization of our relationship to the world that stretches far back historically, culturally, economically, and institutionally but in the twenty-first century has become

newly radicalized, not least as a result of the technological possibilities unleashed by digitalization and by
the demands for optimization and growth produced by
financial market capitalism and unbridled competition.

I will expand upon this phenomenon in greater
detail in what follows. For now, I would simply like to
illustrate it with a few brief examples. Let us consider
our relationship to our own body. Everything that we
perceive about it tends to be subject to the pressures
of optimization. We climb onto the scale: we should
lose weight. We look into the mirror: we have to get
rid of that pimple, those wrinkles. We take our blood
pressure: it should be lower. We track our steps: we
should walk more. Our insulin level, our bustline: we
invariably encounter such things as a challenge to do
better, even if it is a challenge we can ignore or reject.
Moreover, we ought to be calmer, more relaxed, more
mindful, more environmentally conscious. Even those
things we encounter outside ourselves take on the character of a challenge: Mountains have to be scaled, tests
passed, career ladders climbed, lovers conquered, places
visited and photographed ("You have to see it!"), books
read, films watched, and so on. This attitude can even be
found—not just latently, but manifestly—in situations
where we don't appear to be bent on "conquest" at all.
Patrons of the famous German tourist bar Ballermann 6
on Mallorca "destroy" buckets of beer and sangria,
while members of church choirs have to flawlessly
"master Mendelssohn." More and more, for the average
late modern subject in the "developed" western world,
everyday life revolves around and amounts to nothing more than tackling an ever-growing to-do list. The
entries on this list constitute the points of aggression

that we encounter as the world: grocery shopping, checking in on a sickly relative, doctors' appointments, work, birthday parties, yoga classes—all matters to be settled, attended to, mastered, completed, resolved, gotten out of the way.

At this point we are surely inclined to wonder: Isn't this normal? Haven't things always been this way? Haven't human beings always encountered the world and reality as *resistance*?[4] My theory is that the normalization and naturalization of our aggressive relationship to the world is the result of a social formation, three centuries in the making, that is based on the structural principle of dynamic stabilization and on the cultural principle of relentlessly expanding humanity's reach. This may sound complicated, but the basic ideas are very simple. In my view, the character and dynamics of a social formation can only be understood in terms of the interplay between the structures and institutions that constitute it and the cultural forces that drive it: its fears, promises, and desires. The first—the structural dimension—can well be described using the means of empirical scientific observation, that is, from a *third-person perspective*, such as we use to observe and describe, say, the orbits of the planets. What this perspective is incapable of capturing, however, is the dynamic, energetic aspects of society. Social life plays out, and social change occurs, solely on the basis of the hopes and fears of the people who live in a certain formation; and these driving forces, these promises and apprehensions, can be reconstructed hermeneutically, in cultural terms, only from a *first-person perspective*. I have elaborated both my structural and my cultural analysis of modernity at great length in a number of previous books.[5] Here, then, I would like to offer only a brief summary.

Since the eighteenth century, life in the modern, "western" world has undergone a structural change at every level, as a result of which the basic institutional structure of modern society can be maintained only through constant escalation. *A modern society, as I define it, is one that can stabilize itself only dynamically, in other words one that requires constant economic growth, technological acceleration, and cultural innovation in order to maintain its institutional status quo.* In terms of cultural perception, this escalatory perspective has gradually turned from a promise into a threat. Growth, acceleration, and innovation no longer seem to assure us that life will always get better; they have come instead to be seen as an apocalyptic, claustrophobic menace. If we fail to be better, faster, more creative, more efficient, and so on, we will lose our jobs, businesses will close, tax revenues will decline while expenditures increase, there will be budget crises, we won't be able to maintain our healthcare system, our pension levels, and our cultural institutions, the scope of potential political action will grow ever narrower, and in the end the entire political system will appear to have lost its legitimacy. All this can be observed in the early twenty-first century, for example in Greece, which has been plagued by a prolonged recession. At both the individual and the collective level, what generates this will to escalation is not the promise of improvement in our quality of life, but the unbridled threat that we will lose what we have already attained. To argue that modernity is driven by an increasing demand—*higher, faster, farther*—is to misunderstand its structural reality. This game of escalation is perpetuated not by a lust for more, but by the fear of having *less and less*. It is never enough not because we are insatiable, but because we are, always and everywhere, moving down the escalator. Whenever and wherever we stop to take a break, we lose ground against a highly dynamic environment, with which we are always in competition. There are no longer any niches or plateaus that allow us even to pause, let alone say "that's enough." This can be seen empirically in the fact that a majority of parents in the "developed" world report that they are no longer motivated by the hope that their children will have it better than they do, but by the desire to do everything they possibly can *so that they don't have it worse*.

Because modern societies can stabilize themselves only dynamically, that is, through escalation, they are structurally and institutionally compelled to bring more and more of the world under control and within reach, technologically, economically, and politically: to develop resources, open markets, activate social and psychological potentials, enhance technological capabilities, deepen knowledge bases, improve possibilities of control, and so on.

Meanwhile, it would be a grave misunderstanding to see the fear of falling behind as the sole motivational resource behind modernity's compulsion toward expansion. No social formation can persist for very long (particularly not as robustly and resiliently as capitalist modernity has) if it is based only on fear. Hence there must be a second—positive, attractive—force in play, one that we can identify as the promise of *expanding our share of the world*.[6] The tremendously powerful idea that the key to a good life, a better life, lies in expanding our share of the world has arisen as a cultural correlate to the structural logic of dynamic stabilization in modernity's understanding of itself, working its way deep into the tiniest pores of our psychological and emotional life. *Our life will be better if we manage to bring more world within our reach*: this is the mantra of modern life, unspoken but relentlessly reiterated and reified in our actions and behavior. As I would like to demonstrate in this essay, the categorical imperative of late modernity—*Always act in such a way that your share of the world is increased*—has become the dominant principle behind our decision-making in all areas of life and across all ages, from toddlers to the elderly. This explains what makes money so attractive. How much world lies within our reach can be determined directly from our bank account. If our balance is high, then that South Seas cruise, the weekend cabin in the Alps, the luxury apartment in Winterhude outside Hamburg, the Ferrari, the diamond necklace, the Steinway piano, even an Ayurveda retreat in southern India or a secure guided tour of Mount Everest all lie within our reach. If we are billionaires, even a flight to the moon or to Mars is not out of the question. On the other hand, if we are deep in debt, we may not even be able to afford the bus ride home, a sandwich for lunch, or our basement apartment anymore. They are out of our financial reach.

Amazingly enough, the promise of increasing the radius of what is visible, accessible, and attainable to us may explain even the motivation that drives the entire history of technology. This becomes immediately comprehensible if we think about how we expand our individual radius over time via our mode of transportation. Learning to ride a bike is often a defining moment in the evolution of most children's relationship to the world. Why? Because our first bike drastically expands the horizon of what we can reach on our own, of our own volition. *Now I can ride to the lake, to the woods at the edge of town—"my" world is now noticeably bigger.* At least for children living in the countryside, this experience is then repeated step by step, first with their first motorbike or moped—bringing the next village within reach—and then of course with their driver's license and first car, which brings within their everyday individual reach the nearest major city, with all its promises and temptations. Finally, with airplanes, London, Rio, and Tokyo all appear on the horizon of the reachable and, with rockets, the moon, even if this latter is of course not an everyday experience. The story is no different with broadcast media. Radio and television bring "the voice of Berlin" and the city of Tokyo respectively within our acoustic and visual horizon, making the world audible and visible. And, while the telephone extends our acoustic reach only as much as the radio does—but at an individual level—smartphones complete the movement, ushering in an unbelievable expansion of our share of the world. Not only are all our friends and acquaintances, our loved ones and our not so loved ones, now always just a "click" away, we also have all the knowledge in the world—every song, every film, every image, every bit of data that has been digitized—in close proximity at all times. We literally carry it on our person. The world is now at our fingertips in a historically unprecedented way.[7] The idea, or rather the conviction correlated with these processes—that *life comes down to bringing the world within reach*—is inscribed in our bodies and in our psychological and emotional dispositions. This explains the attractiveness not only of money and technology, but also of big cities. Even as many people maintain that they would "much rather" live in the country, a longing served by popular books and magazines with titles like *Country Living* and *The Dirty Life*, human beings worldwide are increasingly being drawn to metropolises and urban centers, and it would be short-sighted in the extreme to perceive economic benefits (such as better jobs or greater convenience) as the *sole* reason for this trend. People, particularly young people, want to live in cities because cities have museums and theaters, shopping centers and cinemas, stadiums and nightclubs, concert arenas and opera houses, zoos and botanical gardens, train stations and subway systems, and much more. Theaters and museums along with football stadiums and zoos are attractive even to those who never set foot in them, because *they have them within reach, almost within walking distance,* and it is the awareness that all these worlds are reachable and accessible at all times that makes the city appear to be a place of rich life. And it is not least the urge to access new worlds that motivates and drives us to learn new abilities and skills. This applies not only to formal degrees such as a high school diploma, which opens to us any number of career options and further educational opportunities, but also to hobbies such as learning a foreign language. *Learn Spanish or Chinese and you will have access to a huge new segment of world that includes not only the people with whom you will be able to speak, but also books, magazines, and websites that you will be capable of reading, institutions and practices that will now be open to you, and so on.* The world of mountain climbing, the world of the high seas, the world of tango, the world of the penguins, the world of shopping in Dubai: all these phenomenal realms present themselves to us as segments of world that are worth "conquering" or "appropriating" in some way, because doing so will "broaden our horizons."

The sociocultural formation of modernity thus turns out to be, in a way, doubly calibrated for the strategy of making the world controllable. We are structurally compelled (from without) and culturally driven (from within) to turn the world into a point of aggression. It appears to us as something to be known, exploited, attained, appropriated, mastered, and controlled. And often this is not just about bringing things—segments of world—within reach, but about making them faster, easier, cheaper, more efficient, less resistant, more reliably controllable.

2
Four Dimensions of Controllability

Upon closer inspection, it quickly becomes apparent that making the world controllable is not a homogeneous process, but one that consists of at least four different elements or can be divided along four dimensions.

(1) Making the world controllable means, first, making it *visible*, that is, making it knowable, expanding our knowledge of *what is there*. And so we use telescopes to peer ever farther into outer space, microscopes to look ever deeper and more closely into the smallest matter, and electric light to make the world visible and thus controllable even at night.[1]

(2) Making the world controllable means, furthermore, making it physically *reachable* or *accessible*. The moon can be reached via rockets, deep space via satellites, the deep ocean via submarines, cellular structures via microtechnology, and the sunken worlds of the past via archaeology. In precisely this sense, the goal of early modern seafarers, beginning

with Columbus, consisted in physically expanding the known European world by making new parts of the world visible and reachable—a program that can absolutely be understood as a "land grab" in the physical sense.[2]

(3) Inextricably linked with this is the third dimension of bringing the world under control, namely by making it *manageable*. The history of colonialism offers an illustrative, tangible example of how the production of knowledge (e.g. in the form of cartography) often goes hand in hand with the expansion of technological and political–military control. Technological innovations, particularly in the areas of transportation and the military, along with the development of infrastructure, made faraway lands penetrable, more easily and more quickly accessible, while political and administrative structures allowed European expansionists to exploit economic resources and to manipulate social processes, often violently. But efforts to bring the world under control are by no means limited to processes of territorial seizure and settlement. The history of our modern relationship to the world is a history of conquering and dominating the night with electric light, the sky with airplanes, the seas with ships, the body with medicine, the temperature of our surroundings with air conditioning, and so on. Scientific analysis, penetration, and comprehension of the mechanisms of causality are a requirement for this form of mastery.

(4) Distinct from this mode of conquering the world technologically and politically, at least in analytical terms, is a fourth dimension of making the world

controllable, namely by making it *useful*, pressing it into service. Here the point is not simply to bring the world under our control, but to make it into an instrument for our own purposes. This also means shaping, designing, producing world. *What is there, what is present* is instrumentalized, transformed into the material and the object of our own projections and desires. This is particularly evident in the field of politics, where election campaigns are invariably waged with promises of enhancement and improvement. *Vote for us and there will be better jobs, higher pensions, better and more affordable housing, faster transportation connections, better schools!*

These four dimensions of making the world controllable —rendering it visible, reachable, manageable, useful —are solidly entrenched in the institutions that form the basis of modern society. *Science*, by its very definition, is concerned with expanding the scope of what is known; the scientific enterprise, according to the formula K-R-K′ (existing knowledge—research—more knowledge), rests on the continually renewed promise of broadening this horizon. *Technology* is then developed in order to make the possibilities and the segments of world disclosed by science manageable, thus bringing the world under our control in all its dimensions. *Economic development*, which follows—or rather is subject to—the capital-driven, escalatory program M-C-M′ (money—commodities—more money), in turn provides the resources, and not only at the societal level but also for individual consumers, who bring the world under their personal control through the acquisition of goods as well as of knowledge and instruments. Finally, *legal regulations* and *political–administrative apparatuses* are charged with managing the social and cultural preconditions and consequences of this program of always expanding our reach—or rather they are charged with ensuring that social processes can be predicted and controlled. The ever-growing accumulation of regulations, provisions, and statutes is the manifest expression of our effort to make social life predictable and controllable in the sense of being justiciable—an effort, however, that is on the verge of failing dramatically, as I will explain in what follows. In fact, the ubiquitous struggle for power can be understood in all respects as a struggle for control: the struggle to expand our share of the world. Whether we are talking about direct authority or command, economic resources, rights of ownership and disposal, or any other form of power, *power always manifests itself in the expansion of one's own share of the world, often at the expense of others.* Indeed, the individual reach of these others is not infrequently brought, partly or entirely, under the control and authority of those with power.

3
The Paradoxical Flipside
The Mysterious Withdrawal of the World

To sum up the argument that I would like to elaborate here, my theory is that this institutionally enforced program, this cultural promise of making the world controllable, not only does not "work" but in fact becomes distorted into its exact opposite. The scientifically, technologically, economically, and politically controllable world mysteriously seems to elude us or to close itself off from us. It withdraws from us, becoming mute and unreadable. Even more, it proves to be threatened and threatening in equal measure, and thus ultimately *constitutively uncontrollable*. The fact that, in late modern culture, we encounter the "world" predominantly in terms of the *environment* or as the "global" of political–economic globalization is a manifest symptom of this development.[1] The former perspective is dominated by our awareness of environmental destruction, the consequences of which increasingly threaten us. The latter perception is no different: in contemporary political discourse, globalization suggests a chaotic, dangerous, uncontrollable outside, which threatens to overwhelm our bounded world of the trusted and familiar, and against this encroachment militarists and protectionists promise to defend us with walls and protective fences, prohibitive tariffs and spring-guns. The world thus appears to be at once uncannily threatened and uncannily threatening—the very opposite of *controllable*.

The world's withdrawal from the grasp of humanity was made vivid during a recent panel discussion in Germany between Erhard Eppler, Niko Paech, and Christiane Grefe.[2] Eppler, asked how he became a critic of economic growth and a pioneer of ecological thinking, answered with a striking and palpable image. Flying over North Africa on one of his first trips abroad as West Germany's minister for economic cooperation, he could see from the airplane how human efforts to clear ever deeper swaths of forest and to settle ever farther up the hillsides had ultimately led, not to the development of fertile new land—in my terminology, to an adaptive transformation of world—but rather to its erosion. The fertile earth, an accommodating, nourishing segment of world, had been washed away, leaving behind an enormous brown carpet where the river flowed out into the sea. In this way, the endeavor to expand our share of the world, to bring the forests and the mountains under our control, had made this exploited segment of world hard, barren, even downright hostile.

But that is not all. At a cultural level, fear of a loss of world in the sense of the world's falling mute, becoming gray and colorless, has accompanied modernity's reach-expanding program from the beginning; indeed, loss of world constitutes the fundamental *basic anxiety* of modernity. It is there even at the beginning of the otherwise so sober, third-person-focused discipline of sociology, in the early writings of Karl Marx, whose thinking in the *Economic and Philosophic Manuscripts of 1844* is animated by his observation of man's fivefold alienation from all facets of the world he encounters. According to Marx, man's relation to the world is defined by the fact that we must "work up" world (i.e. the natural world that surrounds us) in order to appropriate it for ourselves, to nourish, clothe, and shelter ourselves. Unlike with other living beings, the elementary process of metabolic exchange between humans and nature is mediated by labor, by reshaping nature. World thus first appears to us as something to be worked up. But, in working on nature, the subject at the same time forms and, in a way, even generates itself. Human beings, so formed, have also changed in the course of our historical development with the accumulation of productive forces, of the knowledge and instruments that aid us in working up nature. Hence this process is not one of simply "appropriating" nature; rather it is, literally, an *adaptive transformation*. Through labor we form and transform ourselves, our environment, and the process of metabolic exchange itself. In modernity, however, according to Marx, this process of adaptive transformation has been fundamentally disturbed: now world (in the form of raw materials, the products we manufacture, and the goods we consume) is no longer adaptively transformed, but only appropriated. Because laborers under capitalist conditions do not own what they produce, they are alienated from the products of their labor. Moreover, because they are not able to determine the aims, means, and forms of production, they are also alienated from the process of labor, that is, from the very process that forms and constitutes their entire being. Finally, they are alienated from nature, which they confront only as raw material to be economized, as objects to be molded and designed. Just how fundamental alienation is for Marx can be seen from his adoption of William Petty's maxim that labor is the father, land or nature the mother of man; thus we are dealing here with being estranged from both our father and our mother at once.[3] In Marx's view, the core of our existence, our encounter with ourselves and with the world through labor, has become merely an external means of existence, a way of making money. Even more, we are alienated in our relation to the social world as well. Because we, as human beings, find ourselves in constant existential competition with one another, we encounter one another primarily as competitors, and thus with latent hostility; and, over time, this leads to irresolvable self-alienation. Marx thus shares my view that how we relate to ourselves and how we relate to the world are mutually dependent—we cannot have a sound relationship with ourselves if we do not have a sound relationship to the world, and vice versa. If we do not feel ourselves, we cannot adaptively transform the world, and if we encounter the world as mute and numb, we also lose our sense of self. In his later writings, such as *Capital*, Marx proceeds from the assumption that wage labor, arising from the private ownership of the means of production, is the root cause of alienation. The early Marx, however, was deeply ambivalent on this question. Certain passages of the *Economic and Philosophic Manuscripts* read as though an alienated relationship to the world—one in which the world has become a point of aggression—is rather the cause that made possible the establishment of an economic system in which the movement of capital (M-C-M′), considered as a never-ending process of accumulation, could become the true subject of history.[4]

Max Weber, the other great "founding father" of modern sociology, likewise finds it highly irrational that human beings do not work in order to live, but live in order to work and accumulate (in my terminology, to grow, accelerate, and innovate). Yet he understands this relation to the world as part and parcel and the result of a great "western process of rationalization" that unfolds over the centuries and the core of which consists in making life and the world calculable, manageable, and predictable—scientifically, technologically, economically, legally, politically, and finally also in everyday life.[5] This means nothing less than making the world controllable, and Weber identifies this as the flipside of rationalization as a process of progressive alienation, of the world's falling mute, which he describes as a "disenchantment." Weber's at times deeply pessimistic diagnosis is that the world made manageable and predictable has lost not only its color and its magic, but also its voice, its *meaning*. It has "cooled" into a dull "steel-hard shell," within which economic and bureaucratic reason blindly and soullessly advance escalatory processes to the point where human beings have become "nonentities" who "imagine they have attained a stage of humankind never before reached."[6]

In this way, classic sociology can absolutely be understood as an enterprise aimed at analyzing human beings' relationship to the world, an effort to comprehend the culturally, structurally, and institutionally determined —and thus very much *changeable*—ways in which *human beings relate to each other, to things, and to the world as a totality*. This can be seen especially clearly in the work of the third founding father of sociology in Germany, Georg Simmel, who saw analysis of *interactions* as the core task of the discipline. Simmel, too, clearly describes the ambivalence between the expansion of modern individuals' share of the world—which he identifies in part as a process of the expansion of social circles—and a certain change in the quality of the relationship between human beings and the world. In the modern metropolis, he argues, human beings essentially encounter one another in a mode of existential reserve, even latent aversion, that is, with an attitude of "Just leave me alone!" Our primary concern is preventing strangers from getting too close to us. *Keeping one's distance* has become a basic dispositional requirement, though one that carries with it the risk of making us feel isolated even in the midst of the metropolitan masses:

> if I do not deceive myself, the inner aspect of this outer reserve is not only indifference but, more often than we are aware, it is a slight aversion, a mutual strangeness and repulsion, which will break into hatred and fight at the moment of a closer contact, however caused.[7]

This basic mindset is further reflected in the relationship of modern city dwellers to the things and events around them, which they encounter with a "blasé attitude" that today we call "coolness," an attitude of *being unimpressed by anything*:

> The essence of the blasé attitude consists in the blunting of discrimination. This does not mean that the objects are not perceived [. . .] but rather that the meaning and differing values of things, and thereby the things themselves,

The Paradoxical Flipside

are experienced as insubstantial. They appear to the blasé person in an evenly flat and gray tone; no one object deserves preference over any other.[8]

Émile Durkheim, the founder of sociology in France, likewise sees relationlessness—in the sense of being existentially disconnected from other people, from social communities, and from the world in general—as the cause of what he calls *anomie*, the lack of any rules, laws, or standards in social life, which he identifies as the most dangerous form of social pathology. Here, too, the distortion of the pursuit of controllability into its opposite, into total uncontrollability, appears to be the core element of modern ambivalence. This ambivalence is expressed in modern literature even more plainly than in the writings of sociologists. Friedrich Schiller, for example, in his 1788 poem *The Gods of Greece*, uses the strongest metaphors to describe and lament the contrast between an imagined, "expressive," but in many respects uncontrollable ancient world of the gods and a modern world that has been brought under control but at the same time has fallen mute. The former was a world in which "life's blood flowed throughout creation," in which a bond of love connected men, gods, and historical heroes, and the blossoms of nature existed in harmony with the songs of art.[9] The latter, by contrast, is a joyless world, an "empty frame" in which "mournful silence" reigns, an "insensate [. . .] orb of fire" whirling through space, whose woods and waves resound only with empty echoes. Schiller employs dramatic images —"hideous carcasses," "dark shrouds," "shuddering," "the scathing Northern blast"—in order to give expression to the resonancelessness of the modern experience

25

of the world. This experience of alienation from the world finds itself radicalized even further after World War II, for example in Samuel Beckett's *Endgame*. Here the inability to relate to the world is even a physical characteristic of the play's protagonists, who can neither sit nor stand, who have no legs and are blind, and whose vision and hearing are declining while their hair and teeth are falling out. As a result, the question of how these characters are *situated in the world* becomes itself problematic. Living in a dead, "cadaverous and gray" post-apocalyptic world, they have literally lost their standpoint. Here all conceivable axes of resonance have in fact been systematically *muted*. Bodily relationships to the world have been pathologically reduced, nature is dead, physical shelter has taken the form of a dustbin (literally, for two of the characters), and social relationships are marked by incomprehension, repulsion, and contempt. The global catastrophe looming in the background of this one-act drama is nothing but a *terminal catastrophe of resonance*.[10]

On the borderline between philosophy and literature, Albert Camus defines the basic experience of modernity as one of constitutive *hostility* between human beings and the world, in and from which is born the absurd. This hostility bordering on hatred rests on our inability to either know or reach the world—and thus on a fundamental lack of control. For Camus, perceiving the absurd means "perceiving that the world is 'dense,' sensing to what degree a stone is foreign and irreducible to us, with what intensity nature or a landscape can negate us. [. . .] The primitive hostility of the world rises up to face us across millennia."[11] *The absurd* here lies neither in the attitude of the subject nor in the constitution of the world alone, but rather in the relationship between the two. "[T]hat absurdity that determines my relationship with life," Camus writes, "depends as much on man as on the world. For the moment it is all that links them together. It binds them one to the other as only hatred can weld two creatures together."[12] Inner worldlessness and external loss of world—this is how Hannah Arendt characterizes the structure of alienation as an existential *relation of relationlessness*.[13] We may have any number of relationships to the world—a job, strong family ties, maybe political affiliation, religious faith, volunteer work, hobbies—without necessarily feeling alive or connected to them. *None of this means anything to me. It doesn't matter to me, it doesn't affect me, and I'm not having any effect on the outside world.* This experience is characteristic of a depressive condition, when all axes of resonance have fallen mute and "nothing speaks to us anymore." This feeling of a loss of world exists independently of the question of how expansive one's share of the world is. It can arise, individually and collectively, even where—in fact especially where – we have the world technologically, economically, and socially largely in our grasp. *Everything out there is dead, gray, empty, and cold, and everything within me is mute and numb, too.* The fact that this condition, in the form of *burnout*, has now become a fashionable and widespread ailment typical of our time reveals much about modernity's relationship to the world; it is not the frequency of diagnosis (for which there may be many different reasons) that strikes me as significant here, but the fact that even those who are not objectively threatened by either burnout or depression are nevertheless obsessively interested in the phenomenon and *perceive* it to be a threat. My hypothesis is that the fundamental fear of modernity is fear of the world's falling mute, of which burnout and depression are only a timely (and perhaps heightened) expression.[14]

Taking all the above reflections and observations into account, we can note that the individual and institutional efforts of modernity to make the world controllable, in all four dimensions and with an ever wider reach, have yielded paradoxical side effects, which can be described (in the language of Marx) as alienation as opposed to adaptive transformation, as reification rather than revivification (Adorno and Lukács), as loss of world rather than gaining world (Arendt), as the world's becoming unreadable as opposed to comprehensible (Blumenberg), and as disenchantment as opposed to ensoulment (Weber). Modernity stands at risk of *no longer hearing the world* and, for this very reason, losing its sense of itself. This is the conclusion of my sociology of our relationship to the world. Modernity has lost its ability to be *called*, to be *reached*. If we understand this condition in social–philosophical terms, under the rubric of alienation, as a relation of relationlessness, then the question of what a "relation of relatedness to the world" would be takes on not just sociological, but political and practical urgency. What does a successful relationship to the world look like? If the culturally and structurally enforced attitude of conceiving of the world as a point of scientific, technological, economic, and political aggression, as something to be brought within our individual reach, turns out to be the cause of our ever increasing alienation from the world, then the question becomes: What other attitude toward the world is even possible or conceivable? Answering this question

The Paradoxical Flipside

was the aim of my last large-scale work, *Resonance*. In the ensuing chapters I would like to take up again the basic themes of that book in order to show how understanding the relationship between controllability and uncontrollability is of fundamental importance for both understanding the problems of our modern relationship with the world and seeking out potential alternatives to it.

4

The World as a Point of Resonance

Alienation denotes a relation of relationlessness in which subject and world find themselves inwardly unconnected from, indifferent toward, and even hostile to each other. This mode of relation itself contains the seeds of a relation of aggression—though one that, admittedly, first made possible the spectacular successes of scientific, technological, and economic progress. In my reading, the cultural achievement of modernity is that it has nearly perfected human beings' ability to establish a certain distance from the world while at the same time bringing it within our manipulative reach. This sort of aggressive–distancing relationship to the world seems to me indispensable. Our capacity for it appears to be anthropologically innate, a precondition of being a human being, that "eccentrically positioned" creature who not only can but is compelled to distance herself from herself and from her relationship to the world and, in a way, to observe herself from the outside.[1]

The aggressive aspect of our relationship to the world becomes a problem, however, when it begins to permeate every aspect of life, when we forget that subject and world do not simply exist apart from each other as independent entities, but rather emerge first from their mutual relatedness and connection to each other. Subjects are always "in the world," always already involved with, wrapped up in, and related to the world as a whole. "I recognize my affinity with [all beings]," Merleau-Ponty writes. "I am nothing but an ability to echo them, to understand them, to respond to them."[2] Responsivity or capacity for resonance is, in a way, the "essence" not only of human existence, but of all possible manners of relating to the world; it is the necessary precondition of our ability to place the world at a distance and bring it under our control. A capacity for, or rather a dependence on, resonance is constitutive not only of human psychology and sociality, but also of our very corporeality, of the ways we interact with the world tactilely, metabolically, emotionally, and cognitively. The basic mode of vibrant human existence consists not in exerting *control* over things but in resonating with them, making them respond to us—thus experiencing *self-efficacy*—and responding to them in turn. This is what I sought to elaborate in my book *Resonance*, using all available philosophical and scientific means. But how can we define with greater precision this way of relating to the world, in opposition to the mode of aggression and the experiences of alienation that correspond to it? My argument is that resonance is not just a metaphor for a certain experience, or a subjective emotional state, but is a *mode of relation* that can be precisely defined by four exemplary characteristics:

1. *Being affected*. Resonating with another person, or even with a landscape, a melody, or an idea, means being "inwardly" reached, touched, or moved by them. This circumstance of being affected can well be described as a "call" or "appeal." Something suddenly calls to us, moves us from without, and becomes important to us for its own sake. The person or thing from whom or from which we experience such a call appears to us to be not just of instrumental value, but "intrinsically" important. We know we have been affected in this way when, say, our sorrowful countenance abruptly becomes radiant, or when we suddenly find that we have tears in our eyes. Such signs indicate that the shell of reification behind which we usually operate in a world oriented toward escalation, optimization, calculation, and domination has, for a moment, been punctured and we have left the mode of aggression. From a phenomenological perspective, this means that a mode of resonance differs from a state of alienation through a kind of double movement between subject and world. First, the subject is affected by the world, in other words is *touched* or *moved* in such a way as to develop an intrinsic interest in the segment of world so encountered and to feel somehow "addressed."

2. *Self-efficacy*. At the same time, we can speak of true resonance only when this call is followed by our own active *response*. This always manifests itself in a physical reaction that we might describe in everyday language as "getting goosebumps," "the hair on the back our neck standing on end," or "a shiver running down our spine" and that, in medical terms, may be measured as a change in our skin resistance, breathing rate, heart rate,

or blood pressure.³ Resonance also involves our react-
ing to the impulse that calls us by reaching out toward
that which moves us. The word *emotion* is well suited to
describing this second characteristic, as, etymologically,
it denotes a movement outward (from the Latin *emovere*
[= *movere* + the prefix *ex*, "out of"]), a response. From
this perspective, resonance in its full sense occurs only
when we, too, are capable of reaching out to the other
side, when we feel connected to the world because we
ourselves are able to affect something in it (something
that, in turn, also affects us). Hence I call this second
aspect of resonance *self-efficacy*. The simplest version
of such a resonant relationship consists in an exchange
of glances, or in a dialogue in which the two speakers
both listen and respond to each other. Our eyes are
windows of resonance. To look into someone's eyes and
feel them looking back is to resonate with them—that is,
unless we balk at them, warding them off with a hostile
glare or ignoring them with a dead stare. Then we find
ourselves in a state of alienation, a relational mode of
indifference or hostility.

Being reached and addressed by a responding voice
and, conversely, not only making our own voice heard,
but experiencing our voice as having an effect—this
is a fundamental human experience, which precedes
even exchanging glances. It is a life-giving discovery for
infants, as well as one of the promises of democracy
—that is, when the latter is practiced in a mode of
listening and responding rather than of shouting down
and declaring taboo. Of course, we experience ourselves
as simultaneously affecting and being affected, not only
in interpersonal situations but also when we learn how
to play a musical instrument, jump into the ocean to

go swimming, or bake a loaf of bread. In a more subtle sense, we can also speak of self-efficacy when, say, we not only read but begin to *process* a book.

3. *Adaptive transformation.* Whenever we resonate with another human being, a book, a song, a landscape, an idea, a piece of wood, we are transformed by the encounter, although of course in very different ways. There are encounters that leave us "a different person" in their wake, and there are adaptive transformations that produce barely noticeable, often only temporary changes, for example in our voice. In every instance, however, a change in how we relate to the world is constitutive of resonant experience. When we resonate with the world, we are no longer the same afterwards. Experiencing resonance *transforms* us, and it is precisely this transformation that makes us feel alive. If we no longer allow ourselves to be called or transformed, if we find ourselves no longer able to effectively *respond* to the multitude of voices all around us, then we feel dead inside, petrified, in short: incapable of resonance. It is symptomatic of depression, a state in which all our axes of resonance have fallen mute and grown numb, that nothing touches or moves us anymore. At the same time, we also feel that we ourselves cannot reach anyone, that we are "frozen" and thus incapable of change. *Everything out there is lifeless and dead*, we tell ourselves, *and everything in me is mute and cold*, and no expansion of our share of the world can liberate us from this condition. From this perspective, the feeling of being alive depends, strictly speaking, on adaptive transformation in the sense of a transformation *on both sides*. Even if we wish to leave aside the argument, put

forth by authors such as Philippe Descola and Bruno Latour, that attributing a capacity for resonance to human beings alone and holding everything else in the universe to be mute and "dead" is a highly dubious, one-sided approach peculiar to the modern rationalistic–scientific worldview (along with its corresponding mode of aggression),[4] it is nevertheless evident that resonant experiences also significantly change inanimate objects (if only *for us*). *The mountain I have climbed is different (for me) from the one I only saw from a distance or on television*, and in the same way books, music, languages, and ideas also change in the process of adaptive transformation. Indeed, they are not even available to us as "things in themselves."

Resonant relationships thus change both subjects and the world they encounter in such contexts. Precisely this cannot be said in cases of mere *appropriation*. I can buy and even read a book without its touching, moving, or changing me in any way, and I can pray, attend a concert, climb a mountain, or get married all with the same result. Without the trifecta of af←fect (in the sense of being affected by an other), e→motion (as a self-efficacious response that creates a connection), and adaptive transformation, appropriation remains a *relation of relationlessness*. The fact that there must be some interplay among all three of these aspects makes it clear that—like a violin or guitar—we must be open enough to be affected or changed, while at the same time we must also be closed off enough to respond effectively with our own voice. A person who, for example, has experienced traumatic violence may henceforth resist or balk at any form of touch or contact, while, conversely, someone who is affected by everyone and everything will lose their ability to hear and develop their own voice. Individuals who do not trust their ability to both *affect* and *be affected*, who have either forgotten or never experienced the fact that they are capable of both touching others and eliciting from them an accommodating response, will restrict themselves to encountering the world of people and things only in an aggressive–manipulative mode.

4. *Uncontrollability.* The fourth (and, for this book, critical) aspect of resonant relationships consists in the fact that the "pathological" (or simply *unfortunate*) conditions described above cannot be changed merely through an act of will, that resonance cannot be manufactured or engineered. I describe this as the *uncontrollability* of resonance, which means, first, that there is no method, no seven- or nine-step guide that can guarantee that we will be able to resonate with people or things. Even if we attempt to adjust and arrange all subjective, social, spatial, temporal, and atmospheric background conditions so as to facilitate an experience of resonance, it may yet turn out that our romantic date, the view of the mountains at first light, the music heard from the most expensive seats in the house, all leave us "completely cold," that we will find ourselves unaffected and unable to make a connection. We experience this on Christmas Eve, for example, when we try to shake off the pre-holiday stress, to flip the switch, to be entirely there for our loved ones, to let ourselves be moved by the biblical story, the solemn carols, the Christmas spirit—in short, when we try *to listen and respond*. The risk of alienation is never so great as on this night, although we may have a very similar experi-

ence at that candlelight dinner with our beloved or at
that concert by our favorite star. We can never predict
whether or not resonance will transpire and, if it does,
how long it will last. Resonance is inherently uncontrollable. Just as with falling asleep, the harder we try to
make it happen, the less we succeed. Conversely, however, uncontrollability also means that (again as with
falling asleep) having a resonant experience can never
be ruled out entirely. Resonance *can* emerge even under
adverse or radically alienating conditions, even if this is,
of course, unlikely. It is a peculiar characteristic of resonance that it can be neither *forced* nor *prevented* with
absolute certainty.

Resonance is inherently uncontrollable also in a
second, more important sense. Whenever it occurs,
we are transformed; but it is impossible for us to predict how exactly we will be changed and what the end
result of this transformation will be. Until the process
of adaptive transformation is completed, we fundamentally cannot know in what way or how deeply we will
be changed when we really get involved with another
person, another form of life, an idea, a book, or a landscape. This means, however, that the transformative
effects of a resonant relationship always and inevitably
elude any planning on the part of subjects. They can be
neither predicted nor controlled, and this makes them
particularly important to a critique of controllability
such as the one I am elaborating here. Because resonance is inherently *open-ended* in terms of its results, it
is fundamentally in tension both with the social logic of
relentless escalation and optimization and with the corresponding attitude of constantly perceiving the world as
a point of aggression. The uncontrollability of resonance

further means that it cannot be accumulated, saved, or instrumentally enhanced. Anyone who has tried play-ing their favorite song ten times in a row day after day knows this well, as does anyone who has attempted to preserve the resonant potential of an intense moment in a digital photo. Uncontrollability implies, moreover, that we cannot fight or compete for resonance. As soon as we enter into a combative relationship or switch to an aggressive mode, we close ourselves off, dampening the possibility of resonance. We no longer want to be reached, but rather to *assert* ourselves; we aim to experi-ence self-efficacy not by affecting and being affected, but by instrumentalizing and manipulating other people and things. We can purchase an expensive cruise or African safari, but resonance with nature cannot be bought. Advertising and commodity capitalism in general work by translating our existential need for resonance, our *desire for relationships*, into a *desire for objects*. We purchase commodities (cruises, safaris) and hope to experience resonance with nature, but while the former can be guaranteed, the latter cannot, and may even become more unlikely the more we strive to engineer it. *Yes, we want to see the lions, guaranteed, but there is no guarantee that they will approach us, and it can't take too long, because we want to be back in time for dinner, and we don't want to get sunburned or get caught in the rain.*

My sociological theory, as elaborated above, is that modernity is culturally geared and, given how its insti-tutions are designed, structurally driven toward making the world calculable, manageable, predictable, and con-trollable in every possible respect. Yet resonance cannot be made controllable through scientific knowledge, technical mastery, political management, economic efficiency, and so on. That is the great aggravation inherent in this social formation, its *essential contradiction*, which produces ever new waves of enraged citizens. My goal in the second half of this book is to track this fundamental contradiction, in all its various manifestations and all its social and psychological consequences, even in places where we might not expect to find it, in our everyday actions as well as in areas of social conflict. In doing so, I hope to shine a light on the difficulties in which modernity finds itself, not just in its relation to nature but also in its political and subjective relationship to the world and with itself. My second goal in patiently delineating the fault lines and tensions between our desire for resonance and our demand for controllability is to develop some ideas about how this contradiction might be resolved or overcome in the future.

5

Five Theses on the Controllability of Things and the Uncontrollability of Experience

A closer analysis of the relation between resonance and uncontrollability quickly makes it clear that simply equating the two falls short. In fact we are able to resonate with other people or things only when they are in a way "semicontrollable," when they move between complete controllability and total uncontrollability. More precisely, we need to distinguish between the inherent uncontrollability of resonant *experiences* and the fundamental controllability of the things or people we resonate with. From this, it first appears as though the contradiction between the two could actually be resolved. Modernity is oriented toward making as much "world" controllable as possible, in order to increase the likelihood of uncontrollable, yet longed-for and fulfilling resonant experiences.

Five Theses on the Controllability of Things

THESIS I   The inherent uncontrollability of resonance and the fundamental controllability of things do
not constitute a contradiction per se.

Obviously we are capable of resonating with an other
when it is controllable in *at least one* of the four dimensions discussed in Chapter 2. It is of course more likely
that I will able to resonate with another person or
with a landscape if I come into physical contact with
them, although under certain circumstances an image,
a description, or a recording may suffice. There may
well be connoisseurs like Theodor Adorno, who can
fall in love with a piece of music simply by looking at
its score, but in general we need to have actually *heard*
a musical work or a melody in order for it to resonate
with us. This means that it is impossible to resonate
with things that are completely inaccessible or beyond
any form of control. Hence the desire, and then the
development of various techniques, to make music
controllable and accessible, first by establishing regular, professionalized performance practices and, later,
by capturing sound on recording media. Following the
development of recording technology, many people
who associate music with deep experiences of resonance
began amassing ever larger collections of LPs and CDs.
At a certain point they had the complete works of Bach,
Mozart, Beethoven, or Mahler on their shelf, or every
album by Pink Floyd, the Rolling Stones, the Beatles, or
Fleetwood Mac, so they could count on having access
to or control over them in the sense of having them
within reach (dimension 2 of controllability) whenever the moment of resonance—uncontrollable in the
sense of the Greek word *kairos*, which designates the

exact or perfectly right time—arrived. And now, with modern streaming services, they have convenient access to almost the entirety of known and recorded music, at all times and for a relatively small fee. Millions of titles are available and controllable in this sense. Obviously we could tell parallel, structurally identical stories about the accessibility of texts, books, images, and films. This suggests that the motivation driving modern efforts to expand our reach is in fact nothing but our desire for resonance. Precisely because resonance itself is uncontrollable, the goal is to have "the world" at our disposal whenever the right moment arrives. If I want to speak with you, I don't have to wait until our paths happen to cross again, I can just call you. If I want to listen to Beethoven's Fifth Symphony, I don't have to wait until it is being performed in concert, or even until I'm at home with my music collection; I can immediately download to my smartphone a recording that features masterful playing in the highest audio quality. And if I long to visit Egypt, I can book a flight in the middle of the night, for this very weekend. Thus 24/7 appears to be a logical response to the uncontrollability of resonance. The supposedly fundamental contradiction of modernity would thus seem simply to be resolved. But is there something not quite right with this story?

The theoretical answer to this difficult question, which requires analyzing the form of a resonant relationship, is that resonance always implies bilateral movement. It is not enough that I have access to and can take hold of the world. Resonance demands that I allow myself to be *called*, that I be *affected*, that something reach me from the outside. This suggests that the "muting" of the world discussed in Chapter 3, which means nothing but the disappearance of this experience of being called, is a consequence of unlimited access and control. And in fact, taking a closer phenomenological look at the resonant relationships we have, we can see that not only *experiences*, but also the *things* we encounter must contain an element of uncontrollability. Long-form interviews in which people tell the story of their life are almost always structured around pivotal experiences of resonance that mark biographical turning points. These almost invariably take the form of an *unexpected* encounter: *then I met this person, I read this book, I ended up joining this group, someone brought me to this place, and it changed my life.* Being open to the unexpected—to what I awkwardly, metaphorically refer to here as "being called"—also seems to be a prerequisite of smaller, more everyday experiences of resonance. It is precisely the uncontrollability of that first snowfall or of a sunset that evokes the intensity of the resonant experience potentially associated with it. And this of course applies to every human encounter. Whether or not another person—be it a family member, a friend, a colleague, or a stranger—becomes involved in a dialogically or physically resonant relationship with me is something that I *cannot* control. The fact that the other person could say "no" or "not now" is a precondition of being able to resonate with them at all. We cannot resonate with someone who *always* tells us we are right, who *always* encourages or shares our opinions and fulfills our every wish and desire (the dream of the "love robot"). At best, we can only experience an "echo relationship" with them.[1] Strictly speaking, this is also true of my pet cat. I experience her purring and her trustfulness as events of genuine resonance precisely because she can also evade me, because sometimes she *doesn't* purr, but scratches or even bites me—in short, precisely because I cannot completely control her. My argument is that, if I could make it snow at will, then I could never experience being called by the falling snow. If my cat were a programmable robot that always purred and wanted to be cuddled, she would become nothing to me but a dead thing. In another sense, this also applies, say, to a poem that I feel *has something to say to me*. A poem can resonate with me only as long as I have not yet *fully* grasped, understood, and processed it (dimension 3), only as long as it continues to occupy me and still seems to be hiding something from me.

Hence, despite not being able to fully demonstrate it here argumentatively, it seems to me that there must be an aspect of *inherent uncontrollability* not only in our experiences or in our relationship to the world, but also *in things themselves*, if we are to be able to enter into a resonant relationship with them.

THESIS 2   Things we can completely control in all four dimensions lose their resonant quality. Resonance thus implies semicontrollability.

My theory of "semicontrollability" may help to explain why *home* [Heimat] only becomes a resonant concept after we have *already lost it*. As I have sought to show elsewhere,[2] home represents our hope for a segment of world that we can adaptively transform, our desire to find or create a place in the world where things (plants and trees, mountains and streams, bridges and streets, houses and cottages, people and animals) *speak to us*, where they *have something to say to us*. A segment of world loses its resonant quality in this sense if it is completely controllable. Soon enough, it falls silent or bores us. This applies not only to physical segments of world, but also to all kinds of encounters. When we have completely *mastered* something, it no longer has anything to say to us. We are "done with it." When people experience a book—*the Bible*, say, or Marx's *Capital*—as a resonant other, this is only because they feel that they have not yet fully grasped it, because it continues to provoke, or at times even outrage them. To offer a final, highly illustrative example, in an interview with the weekly magazine *Die Zeit*, the famous German Russian pianist Igor Levit was asked whether he could even still listen to the extremely popular first movement of Beethoven's "Moonlight" Sonata. His answer:

> Yes. I played the sonata just recently. The more often I play a sonata, the more I work with it—the less I apprehend it, the more it eludes me, the happier I am with it, the more frequently I want to play it. [. . .] I never want to say, "I've got this. Next, please." The goal is, I always want to arrive back at the beginning.[3]

Not only does Levit here explicitly link his experience of happiness to the sonata's uncontrollability (in the sense of dimension 3), his thoughts also suggest that categorical statements like "I've already heard Beethoven, now I want to listen to something else," or "I've already been to the Alps, now I want to go someplace else," or even "Christmas is always the same, I'm spending the holidays in the South Pacific this year" raise doubts that Beethoven, the Alps, or Christmas ever constituted axes of resonance for the people who say such things. At the same time, Levit's experience makes it clear that *expertise* is certainly not the enemy of resonance. As a pianist, Levit has developed and refined his musical skills in order to make Beethoven's sonata speak in a way, in order to enter into an ever deeper dialogue with it so that both he and it always have something new to say to each other. This is an entirely different form or use of expertise from that of someone who aims only for technical command and mastery of a piece in order to make it technically manageable (dimension 3) and commercially useful (dimension 4).

This is why, to come back to the example of the robotic cat, the uncontrollability inherent in any resonant relationship cannot be produced by a randomization program. If I were greeted in the evening not by my cat, but by a fluffy robot with big adorable eyes, a randomization program could well ensure that, on average, it would want to nuzzle and be petted by me nine times out of ten, while the other ten percent of the time it would hiss and run away from me. This would certainly introduce an element of uncontrollability—in the sense of *unpredictability*—to our "relationship." Could a resonant relationship, then, develop between me and my robot, similar to the one I have with my actual cat? I suspect that this would not occur, at least not in the same way, first because there would be no *responsive relationship* between the robot's behavior and my own. At the very least, if I knew about the randomization program, I would have to interpret the robot's behavior as erratic, and thus non-responsive. I would know that it isn't trying to say anything to me, that it isn't even acknowledging me at all, that its behavior has nothing to do with me. But, to give this speculative fantasy a different spin, let us imagine that the robot is capable of *learning* and adapts its behavior to mine in some way. This, it seems to me, would truly make for a "mute" relationship, as I would then inevitably attempt to figure out what learning mechanisms provoked or produced its behavior.

Erratic uncontrollability not only has nothing to do with resonance but, to the contrary, has the potential to destroy it, evoking experiences of tremendous alienation. Anyone who has ever used a personal computer or tablet knows this well. These devices repeatedly do things that we do not understand, that seem to be *illogical* and *unmotivated*. They resist us in a way that we almost cannot help but see as malicious. It is remarkable just how enraged we can become when a computer defies all of our commands. Why do we find this form of uncontrollability so repulsive? One explanation is surely that a computer's erratic behavior undermines our self-efficacy. We feel completely powerless, which by definition makes resonance impossible. But that is not all. In such moments, we experience the machine's "actions" as genuinely non-responsive, although its interface is designed for dialogue and accommodation. Computers simulate resonance, but only follow algorithms. The cause–effect relationship between our actions and theirs is not "accommodating" but mechanical, and repeatedly proves to be contingent and erratic. The incongruity between simulated resonance and "blind" or "mute" resistance seems to evoke intense frustration and occasionally even blind rage.

This makes it clear, however, that the uncontrollability of our counterpart in a resonant relationship is a *qualified* form of uncontrollability, not a result of mere chance or contingency. We can only resonate with a counterpart that in a way "speaks with its own voice," that has something like its own will or character, or at least its own inner logic that, as such, remains beyond our control. What is more, we must be able to understand this voice as speaking *to us*, and thus as being in some sense responsive. This is what mountain climbers mean when they say that every mountain has "its own character," and why sailors say that you have to listen closely to the sea to understand it.

THESIS 3   Resonance demands a form of uncontrollability that "speaks," that is more than just contingency.

But is snowfall actually uncontrollable in this sense? Does a mountain, even if it has its own character, speak *to me*? It is clear to me that this hypothesis is the most difficult, the murkiest and most controversial, the least demonstrable of all. I would like in this small book to limit myself to the phenomenological side of our relationship to the world, meaning that I do not wish to inquire whether a mountain "itself" speaks (which nobody knows anyway), but only to investigate the kinds of experience we have with and in relation to it. What appears to me to be critically important here is the small, linguistically subtle experiential difference between the statements "This mountain has something to say to me" and "This mountain speaks to me." When people experience resonance with a mountain, a book, a record, or the first snowfall, this means that they have encountered or confronted something that concerns them in some way, that has a meaning for them. Indeed, in everyday language we say things like "This book (or song) appeals to me" to describe even the most banal forms of this sensation. By this we do *not* mean that the book or song in question actually speaks to us in any concrete or metaphysical sense, but rather that we are in some way called by it, and that at the same time we, or something inside us, react and respond to it. Such experiences, however—regardless of whether our counterpart is another person, a piece of music, a mountain, or the falling snow—also involve, first, a feeling of inner change or transformation and, second and foremost, the assumption or hope that it might be worth engaging more closely with that which appeals to us, precisely because we do not fully understand it or have not yet exhausted it. As long as a resonant relationship exists, our counterpart in it remains an other, something foreign to us that continually eludes or resists us, just as Igor Levit so exquisitely describes. Thus resonance can by no means be equated with the experience of "sheer beauty" or "pure harmony." Consonance can certainly be experienced as resonance, but only against the backdrop of an experience of difference. When two different, independent voices temporarily meet or come together, this can indeed evoke an overwhelming experience of resonance, but only as long as we consciously perceive the other *as* an (uncontrollable) other.

This does not mean that the other we encounter must have its own genuine will; yet experiencing resonance implies something like experiencing an independent (counter)force that resists any form of "mechanical" control. *There is something about this mountain, this painting, this tree,* we tend to say, and this something can make demands on us. We must engage with it if we want to truly encounter it. And, with this, we begin perhaps instinctively to understand why Schopenhauer saw all things as possessing a *will*.[4] The concept of *willfulness* is perhaps best suited to conceptualizing this idea. It is the *willfulness* of Beethoven's "Moonlight" Sonata that Igor Levit senses, that he enters into a mutual relationship with, that repeatedly eludes him; and the mountain climber's relationship with the mountain is no different. Resonance means nothing other than that this willfulness is not simply fixed but changes dynamically, particularly in our encounter with it. What a book, the "Moonlight" Sonata, or the Matterhorn *says* to us also depends on how we respond to it. The third characteristic of a resonant relationship implies that *both* sides are continually transformed. For Charles Taylor, the fundamental achievement of the philosophy and poetry of German romanticism, as encountered in the work of Hölderlin, Friedrich and August Schlegel, Novalis, and Schelling, was making it possible to conceive of reality as being co-constituted in this way, in a mutual movement between subject and world.[5] More contemporary philosophical and even physical approaches (new materialism, for example) aimed at elaborating relational ontologies have further developed this idea in modern epistemological terms.[6] For the purposes of this book, however, it will be enough to analyze just the phenomenological side of the relationship between subject and world, that is, the ways in which we, as subjects, encounter and experience the world.

Fatally, it is precisely our sense that we are *not yet finished* with something, that *there is still something there*, that tempts us into trying to "take hold" of it in order to bring it under our control, to be able to access and engage with it at will. Our efforts to secure "resonant" encounters medially, especially by photographing or filming them, are a particularly revealing example of this. Such media make it possible for us to take naturally ephemeral phenomena such as snowfalls and sunsets "out of time," making them accessible and controllable for the future. Unfortunately, however, attempting to take hold of the dynamic of resonance generally means *paralyzing* it. When we approach a landscape, an event, or an object with the eye of a photographer, these things stop speaking to us. We may well be able to sense that a landscape *would have* something to say to us, which is why we want to take hold of it in the first place, but it does not speak to us when we fix our photographic gaze on it or capture it on film. This observation is difficult to prove empirically, but anyone can experience it for themselves at any time. Reaching for a camera shifts the focus of our attention as well as the attitude with which we encounter the world. When we look at the camera display—or rather even before this, when we recognize someone or something as potentially photogenic—we adopt an attitude aimed at freezing part of the world's potential, so to speak ("there is something"), in order to be able to take hold of it. In the language of Erich Fromm, this can be understood as a shift from a mode of existence oriented toward *being* to one oriented toward *having*. Fromm's analysis of the difference between an attitude of dynamic and open spontaneity and one of fixating and accumulative control comes astonishingly close to my own distinction between resonant and mute relationships to the world.[7] From this can be derived my fourth thesis:

THESIS 4 An attitude aimed at taking hold of a segment of world, mastering it, and making it controllable is incompatible with an orientation toward resonance. Such an attitude destroys any experience of resonance by paralyzing its intrinsic dynamism.

The subtle difference between a relationship to the world that is not only shaped by, but draws its very power from, a relation of dynamic openness between subject and world and one that attempts to eliminate the uncertainty associated with this openness (which brings along with it certain risks) is captured more clearly than we might think in our own habitual physical reactions. It can be seen not only in the change in our physical *relatedness to the world* when we reach for our camera but also, and perhaps even more palpably, when we are playing music or sports, in those moments when we suddenly realize that we are not in full control of what we are doing and then attempt to take control over our subsequent movements. Any pianist, for example, knows that subtle tipping point moment, when she is playing a piece—perhaps from memory—and her fingers seem to be finding the right keys all on their own. Suddenly she realizes that she is not in control of her playing and, by consciously trying to take control, she senses that she is about to make a mistake and fall out of this dynamic equilibrium. The same thing happens to tennis players, too, when they start *thinking* about what to do with the next ball.

Conversely, in my view, the phenomenon of procrastination, which especially haunts writers, can best be explained by the fact that we know that the question of whether or not we will successfully manage to write something, whether we will resonate with the text or object at hand, depends neither on our will nor on our effort. Our fear that we will be unable to capture the *willfulness* of the text because we are "not in the right mood" prevents us from even attempting to do so. We cannot approach the still unwritten text, as we do most of the other tasks on our to-do list, as a point of aggression, or least not only as such; we cannot simply "get it out of the way." Perhaps the fact that we are so unaccustomed to adopting a different attitude toward accomplishing "tasks," one that would be sensitive to resonance, is the reason why psychosocial counselors at universities are nowadays overrun with suffering procrastinators.[8]

These last examples demonstrate that it is not enough to focus just on the subject side of experience or on the object side of things (or on both) in defining the relation between controllability and uncontrollability. The uncontrollability constitutive of resonant relationships in fact has a subject dimension, an object dimension, and a *process dimension.* As we have already seen, uncontrollability on the side of the *subject* means that we must be willing to allow ourselves to be touched and changed in unpredictable ways. Resonance implies vulnerability and a willingness to make ourselves vulnerable. On the *object* side, uncontrollability means that what we encounter must resist us in at least one of the four dimensions of calculation and control. There must be at least one "obstinate remainder" that *has something to say to us,* that is meaningful to us in the sense of a *strong evaluation.* Another person, the "Moonlight" Sonata, a poem, a text we are trying to read or write, or a mountain can all be objects or—in the terminology of my book *Resonance*—axes of resonance for us in this sense. But what exactly happens when we try to resonate with this person, this poem, or this text, or (insofar as resonance implies a passive experience of "being called") when they resonate with us? This is the very question addressed in Chapter 2, and my answer to it is the four characteristics of resonant relationships identified there. However, it is also worth applying the last of these, the category of uncontrollability, back to the other three. First, what I have referred to as being "called" or affected is beyond our control. It might happen that I read my favorite poem and suddenly it says nothing to me; I cannot *find my way into it*. The same thing can also happen with my favorite music, or with a conversation with my best friend, or with the text I am trying to write. The question that intrudes upon us in such moments is, "What is the point of all this?"

Scholars of the phenomenon of self-efficacy distinguish between our expectations and our experience of it.[9] If I do not expect to be capable of writing a book, or playing soccer, or "getting into" poetry, then I will not be able to resonate with these activities. To the contrary, I will quickly become convinced that writing or soccer or poetry *doesn't speak to me*. Meanwhile, whether I manage to resonate with something *this time* or *today* is precisely one of those inherent uncontrollabilities that persist even when my expectations of self-efficacy are justifiably high. Let it be noted here that, in the context of resonance theory, self-efficacy does *not* mean having control over the process or result of a given activity, but rather being able to reach something or someone as part of a responsive, open-ended encounter. When we engage in activities in which we are certain of the outcome, we may well experience success, but never resonance. Mihaly Csikszentmihalyi develops precisely this idea in his comprehensive theory of the experience of "flow."[10] According to Csikszentmihalyi, flow—which we can certainly interpret here approximately as an experience of resonance—occurs when we engage in activities in which we feel neither overwhelmed nor underchallenged. In the former case, we would lack self-efficacy; in the latter, the very certainty of our success would prevent us from experiencing resonance. Hence, here again, the admittedly awkward term "semicontrollability"[11] seems to hit on just what it is that makes resonance possible. Musicians experience it when they improvise together;[12] journalists, authors, and scholars, when they write; the members of a soccer team, when they play in competition. In my view, what makes soccer so attractive is precisely the fact that it is far more difficult to control a ball with one's feet than with one's hands. This increases the *uncontrollability* of the game in terms of both the actions of the individual players (e.g. shots or crosses) and the interactions, the "harmony" of the team.[13] Yet acquiring and improving the skills needed to handle the ball not only does not reduce the likelihood of experiencing resonance, but in fact, just as in the case of the pianist discussed above, is apt to enhance the quality of such an experience. The line between what is controllable (in the sense of being "technically possible") and what is uncontrollable remains intact, but consistently shifts in favor of the former. Semicontrollability is, likewise, what lures mountain climbers to the highest and steepest cliffs (although these admittedly also lend themselves to a reifying attitude of conquest) and what compels hikers to set out into the wilderness. Even if they know the route well, the appeal of hiking lies in the moments that cannot be controlled, in small, unexpected encounters.

The ideas developed in this chapter, often only by way of illustrative examples, can perhaps best be conceptualized in terms of a distinction between *reachability* and *controllability*, which can be applied in turn to the experiencing subject, the object or counterpart encountered by said subject, and the interaction between the two. For the subject, being reachable means being fundamentally capable of being touched, of being *called*, such that resonance may occur. As we have seen, however, subjects cannot control their capacity for resonance. *Today I will allow myself to be touched! I intend to be moved by my date tonight!* Neither of these statements represents a viable plan, no matter how often we try to schedule such a "call" at a specific date and time—Christmas Eve! Candlelight dinner!—or to acquire the right to it, so to speak, by commodifying it. *I bought expensive concert tickets for tonight! I paid for an exclusive safari, so I'm entitled to the corresponding experience!* At the same time, reachability is not a matter of pure contingency. We can of course try to create the dispositional and situational conditions necessary for us to be capable of being moved. A museum, for instance, is a place where we generally do not pursue any instrumental aims, where we want instead to come into contact with things in a way that is geared not toward escalation or control, but toward unexpected or unpredictable, resonant encounters, where we are inwardly open and ready to be called.

As we have seen, the same applies to the objects we

encounter. Resonance is impossible if we cannot reach or access them in some form (we must able to read the Bible or Marx's *Capital*, or hear a piece of music, in order to resonate with it), but equally impossible if they are completely controllable in all four dimensions. In terms of process, the difference between reaching something and controlling it is critical. Reachability implies, first, the fundamental possibility of "making contact," of establishing a meaningful inner connection; second, the experience, or at least expectation, of self-efficacy in the sense of being able to reach the object we come into contact with; and, third, an element of responsivity in the mutual interaction between self and world, which in a resonant experience seem to answer or react to each other in an "expressive," meaningful way. This applies even when said meaning essentially remains concealed from us or from outside observers. Any effort to direct or optimize an interaction with respect to its outcome (whether in the context of caregiving, education, scholarship, or even politics) results in the muting of the axis of resonance in question. This is the essence of what I described above as the uncontrollable aspect of resonance. Resonance requires giving up control over both what we encounter and the process of encountering it, and at the same time being able—and trusting in our ability—to reach out to this other side and establish responsive contact with it.

The basic conflict of modernity, which I identified in the previous chapter, consists in mistaking reachability for controllability. Modernity not only is geared toward confusing these two categories in all three dimensions, it is compelled to convert the former into the latter: in processes of self-optimization, in the progressive domination of the world through technology, and in the process-related maximization of output.

THESIS 5   Resonance requires a world that can be reached, not one that can be limitlessly controlled. The confusion between reachability and controllability lies at the root of the muting of the world in modernity.

It is perhaps no coincidence that the concept of uncontrollability originates in the context of theology, where it encapsulates a fundamental element of human beings' relationship with the world—an element that, leaving aside any and all theological or metaphysical assumptions about the nature of God (or even whether there is a God), is also of sociological, philosophical, and psychological interest. As Hermann Deuser has shown, the German term *Unverfügbarkeit*—the "uncontrollability" of this book's title—was coined in the 1930s by Rudolf Bultmann in his work on Kierkgaard's existential philosophy and, from the beginning, was used in opposition to ideas that suggested that the world, human beings, and life itself could be brought under complete technological control.[14] In my layman's understanding, the essence of the Judeo-Christian conception of God consists in an idea entirely in keeping with resonance theory. Even if—and especially if—God is conceived of in generally negative theological terms, as fundamentally *inaccessible* or *beyond control*, the relationship between God and the human being is understood to be one of mutual relatedness and reachability. Humans are supposed to *listen* to God or *hear* God's word, and God in turn can be reached through prayer—although this precisely does not mean that he can in any way be controlled. Leaving aside any and all endless theological debates,[15] responsivity here signifies an ultimate, potentially transformative relationship of mutual listening that also allows each side its "own voice" and freedom to respond. Whether resonance occurs or what its result might be remains uncontrollably open. In my view, this kind of relatedness forms the basis of the practice of prayer, which cannot be understood otherwise. In contrast to what happens in the practices of alchemy or magic, in prayer there is no attempt to manipulate the other side or to engineer a particular result. The aim is rather to feel or sense an accommodating response, the content of which is not predetermined.

Here again, however, uncontrollability does not simply mean contingency. Religious concepts such as grace or the gift of God suggest that accommodation cannot be *earned*, demanded, or compelled, but rather is rooted in an attitude of approachability to which the subject-as-recipient can contribute insofar as he or she must be receptive to God's gift or grace.[16] In sociological terms, this means that resonance always has the character of a *gift*, of something that is bestowed upon or befalls us. The inherent uncontrollability of resonance implies exactly this.

Having attempted, however tentatively and abstractly, to define the relation between the controllable and the uncontrollable in resonant relationships, we can now return to our analysis of the basic conflict between our efforts to make the world controllable and our longing to resonate with it. In the next chapter I would like to pursue this theme through a series of practical contexts and life stages that reveal ever new facets of the complex of problems that result from this conflict.

———

6

To Take Control or to Let Things Happen?

The Basic Conflict of Modernity at Six Stages of Life

The irresolvable tension between our efforts and desire to make things and events predictable, manageable, and controllable and our intuition or longing to simply let "life" happen, to listen to it and then respond to it spontaneously and creatively, can be found in nearly all life processes and at every stage of life, from birth to death. Although it might not be particularly helpful in terms of categorially conceptualizing the problems associated with this tension, I would like nonetheless to take the liberty in this chapter of simply following the chronology of life from this perspective.

Birth

The birth of a human being is in fact a field of conflict between control-oriented and resonance-oriented approaches, and this in three respects. The first concerns the matter of planning for and being able to realize one's desire to have children. Prior to the invention of modern contraceptives, becoming pregnant and being "blessed with children" was to a large degree uncontrollable; abortion represented a questionable attempt to take control of events after the fact, and exacted a high price on all sides. Today, however, pregnancy has moved entirely into the realm of the plannable, calculable, and predictable. When is the "right time" in life to have children? With the advent of "social freezing," that is, of the ability to extract and freeze human egg cells until a later, more convenient date, even the age at which a woman becomes a mother is controllable. Of course, this form of control has its weaknesses, at both ends. First, children can always be conceived unexpectedly or ahead of schedule; conversely, women frequently do not become pregnant even when they and their partner desire to. There is still something palpably uncontrollable about the emergence of new life, although we are now hard on its heels, thanks to the methods of modern reproductive medicine. From in vitro fertilization to surrogate motherhood to expanding adoption rights, modern society has found ways to make children more "accessible." Childlessness or having an abundance of children is no longer a "fate" given to us as a kind of task or challenge to which we must listen and respond in terms of how we live our lives; it is instead either a plan or a mistake. Let me not be misunderstood: I in no way mean to say here that things were good before and are bad now. In past eras, either being "blessed with children" or failing to produce offspring could have literally fatal consequences, destroying any possibility of resonance. I simply want to point out that here something of existential significance has migrated from the realm of the uncontrollable into that of the controllable; and, as I have sought to show, this is neither good nor bad per se.

The second, ethical front line between controllability and uncontrollability that runs through the field of natality concerns the question of a child's or embryo's genetic or biological "quality." Until only very recently, whether a child was born "healthy" or "sick" according to contemporary standards was a matter of fate entirely beyond our control. Today, however, embryo screenings, amniotic fluid tests, and various other methods of medical examination allow us to determine, even before birth, whether a child meets our expectations—and, if not, to end its life. Life and death really have been made engineerable here; the degree of disability we are willing to accept can be calculated and controlled, and we now appear to be not very far away from potentially being able to control our children's physical characteristics, and perhaps even their personality traits. I do not wish to join the chorus of all those who see such examples as only clarifying just how ethically problematic these developments are, and as indicating that we would do better to leave well enough alone. My interest here is sociological. Doubly planned births demonstrate the extent to which we have expanded our medical and personal reach into the world, bringing previously uncontrollable phenomena under our control. From an ethical perspective, however, I am also interested in the related question of whether our unwillingness to accept uncontrollability as an essential aspect of resonance reduces our chances of experiencing it. Listening and responding constitute a different attitude from planning, doing, and calculating. If I remain childless despite wanting to have children, I can try to listen to "what life is trying to tell me" and to respond in the form of how I live my life, which in turn will surely change me as a person. (In a similar way, perhaps I could also listen and respond to a disabled child?) But if whether or not I have children, and what kind, lies entirely within my own power and that of my doctors—does this not change my relationship to life overall?[1] A sociologist of course does not need to know what the right answer to this question is—but he must be able to ask it.

In a way, the third front line in the struggle between controllability and uncontrollability runs *through childbirth itself.* For most women, giving birth is an existential experience and in many respects an uncontrollable process—although always more aspects of it can indeed be controlled nowadays. The moment of birth can be radically determined through a Caesarean section or, in a more limited way, through labor-inducing medication, while modern medical devices have made it possible to monitor and to some extent regulate every physiological parameter in both mother and child. And beyond this there are also a multitude of more or less serious physical and psychological techniques, along with an even greater number of guidebooks and courses, all designed to help bring the uncontrollable aspects of this elementary process within reach. The remarkable, paradoxical result of this, however, is greater *anxiety* about childbirth and a heightened perception of the *uncontrollabilities* and risks associated with it, which we experience as powerlessness. Home birth has thus come to be viewed as a major—and "irresponsible"—risk, while greater knowledge of all the potentially problematic processes and parameters over which women in labor have, themselves, no control —because they are reliant on monitors and on the functioning of the associated hard- and software, as well as on the interventions of hospital personnel—has over many years led to a statistical increase in childbirth-related anxiety.[2] This is a similar dynamic to that seen in security technology. The more surveillance cameras, warning devices, burglar alarms, and protective fencing are installed around a property, the less secure residents feel.[3] The lack of effective individual control over something *potentially* controllable evidently transforms uncontrollability into powerlessness and insecurity. Our confidence in our own effectiveness and in our ability to listen and respond to situations appropriately is undermined when these capacities are given over to experts and machines. These two examples illustrate once again that neither uncontrollability nor semicontrollability, by themselves, facilitate successful resonant relationships. What is required is an "accommodating" or "expressive" uncontrollability, along with the possibility of a self-efficacious response.

Child-Rearing and Education

The insecurity that can arise along with an increased knowledge and greater possibilities to intervene in "natural" processes manifests itself just as dramatically when it comes to issues surrounding childhood development and parenting. Here again, it is those parameters of physical and mental development that can be measured, and that in some cases government authorities require to be measured (e.g. height, weight, diet, sensory functions, organ functions, blood values, bone strength, pediatric diseases, physical, mental, and social abilities, etc.), that render controllable the various processes involved in growing up, both in the first dimension (visibility) and, potentially, in the third dimension (intervention and regulation), in order to ensure "age-appropriate development" as well as the early detection of illnesses requiring treatment or of any developmental delays or other "abnormalities." Our children's development is now monitored via a whole series of medical examinations. At the same time, there are also countless guidebooks and support programs aimed at promoting every individual developmental step and steering these steps in the right direction. As in the case of childbirth or home security, here too the measurability and manageability of multiple processes seems not to diminish anxiety but to heighten it. This can be seen in modern parents' concern that their child's every discomfort, every scratch, every abnormality in his or her growth, speech, motor skills, or communicative faculties requires medical attention. This dependence on experts and on medical devices undermines parents' expectations of self-efficacy and, consequently, their ability to experience it. It is no longer parents themselves who listen to their children's needs and then (in resonance with them) seek out an appropriate response, but rather doctors and experts acting on the basis of reliable data, thus making developmental processes as controllable as possible.[4]

The question of whether bodily processes can or should be controlled through medicine and technology ultimately arises with every individual medical intervention, from getting braces to taking antibiotics, and especially when it comes to administering vaccines. The fierce battle that has been waged in recent decades over the issue of whether or not to vaccinate children against pediatric diseases seems to me to define the cultural frontline between an "ideology of control" and an "ideology of resonance with nature." Should children and their bodies find the right responses to such diseases themselves, or should we eliminate otherwise unpredictable dangers through medical intervention? It might seem that, from a resonance theory perspective, one would absolutely have to make the case for the former option. But this conclusion is premature. The tremendous successes modernity has had in making natural processes controllable, both in and beyond the field of medicine, have yielded scientific, technological, medical, and even political advancements that have created, established, and secured spaces of resonance for many people in many different contexts. Medical interventions that preserve or restore people's hearing or vision, to take two extreme examples, can surely be counted as factors that facilitate resonance. Conversely, uncontrollability as such—dying of appendicitis in the absence of medical assistance, for instance—certainly does not deepen one's resonant relationships. Again, the ideas presented here do not constitute an ethical plea. My aim is rather, first, to define the constantly shifting frontlines between those things we want and are able to control and those to which we want and need to find existential answers precisely because they are uncontrollable and, second, to identify the social manifestations of the basic conflict between our desire for control and our longing for resonance.

Our desire to guide and control our children's development goes far beyond physical–medical issues, however. It also manifests itself as the pressure to optimize nearly every aspect of their lives. How can I ensure that my child is maintaining an optimal diet, developing sufficient and appropriate motor skills, sleeping well, speaking correctly, developing her musical and athletic abilities, her intellectual potential, her social and emotional intelligence? All these aspects of development have now been "parameterized," in other words they have been made quantitatively measurable one way or another, and for each one there are countless experts, guidebooks, and support programs. Ironically, the vast majority of these recommend "listening to your child and his needs." But listening is everywhere in competition with the "measuring" and "comparing" of experts, while guidebooks and support programs tend to declare, or at least to suggest, what the proper response should be.

Parameterization of skills development has become the rubric under which education policy and "evidence-based" research on child-rearing seek to make educational processes *measurable* and thus *controllable*.[5] If we understand education as the acquisition of certain skills—and this is the dominant understanding today, both in politics and in academia—then we can use standardized curricula to define with precision what should be learned when, comparative global surveys (such as the triennial PISA study) to measure with precision whether these goals have been reached, and targeted teaching and learning methods, along with accompanying evidence-based academic research, to determine with precision what screws should be turned when in order to improve the results. This at least is the dream of contemporary educational policy—although every teacher knows all too well that education does not work this way. As I have argued elsewhere in multiple publications,[6] education is, at best, a semicontrollable process of establishing resonance between subject and world or between child and a certain segment of world. Education occurs not when a particular skill has been acquired, but when a socially relevant segment of world "begins to speak," that is, when a child or an adolescent suddenly realizes: *Oh! History—or politics, or physics, or music—says something to me. It concerns me in some way, and I can engage with it self-efficaciously.* When exactly this "spark" occurs is effectively uncontrollable. Mostly it happens at unplanned, unexpected, often incidental moments, and just as uncontrollable is what a young person then makes of or does with the segment of world in question (a poem, the Thirty Years War, Kepler's laws, etc.), what it says to him or her. Education is thus a process of continual transformation in which the subject develops into a person with his or her "own voice," a voice that is itself also uncontrollable. Certain skills are helpful and often necessary if we want to make something speak (be it a sonata, a text by Plato, or the intertropical convergence zone), to establish a progressively deeper responsive relationship, the paradigmatic form of which I described here through the example of Igor Levit. But skills development is never the ultimate goal of education; that it has become the goal of educational policy is simply a result of the fact that, unlike education itself, skills can be precisely measured and to a large degree *made controllable*. Consequently the front line between ideologues of control and ideologues of resonance now runs through every school, and especially through every academic discipline concerned with education and child-rearing. At more than a few universities, this front line has become so hardened that the relevant departments and institutions are now split between those who seek to establish hard standards through quantitative measurement and those who seek to advance Humboldtian educational ideals in a more humanistic–hermeneutic way.[7] Meanwhile teachers—who day after day are torn between on the one hand the control demanded by education authorities and standardized curricula, along with the performance expectations of parents, and on the other hand the students' need for resonance, along with the resonant processes that occur in the classroom *regardless*—find themselves more susceptible to *burnout* than any other class of professionals.[8]

Life Planning: Relationships and Careers

Before we finish school, it is primarily our parents, doctors, and other authorities who seek to make our lives and developmental processes controllable (in all four dimensions). Afterwards, as young adults, we try to "get a handle" on our own lives, which most often means finding a career as well as a life partner. Taking control here, at least in theory, generally assumes the form of career management and family planning, and it is worth studying the ways in which the basic conflict of modernity manifests itself in both of these areas of our lives. The question young people probably hear most often in the course of their development is: "What do you want to be when you grow up?" It suggests that the career we later end up in is, or at least should be, our own decision and, as such, a matter of planning—an idea that gives high school graduates veritable panic attacks. Before graduation, their lives frequently seemed to run on a kind of track, with scarcely any opportunities for them to make their own choices. Afterwards the world opens out into the unforeseeable. Should I go straight to college or take a year off? Should I study physics or music? Should I attend university or a vocational school? Should I continue my studies at all? And, if so, where? Here again, an abundance of guidebooks and experts are available whose advice generally goes as follows: (1) meticulously define your needs, desires, and abilities; (2) examine just as meticulously the various educational offerings available at colleges and universities, and consider as well whether you might want to learn a trade, enter into a dual study program that combines academics and vocational training, or study abroad; (3) in addition to this, inform yourself about opportunities for financial support, the price and quality of student housing, and the social services available at the institutions you are considering attending; and (4) make the decision that most closely conforms to your desires, abilities, and needs. The only problem with this is that fulfilling even the first criterion is simply impossible (*I don't know exactly what I want!*), while fulfilling the second would be a lifelong task, and one that could never be completed, not least because the various degree programs offered by colleges and universities, along with the requirements for completing them, change more rapidly than even the fastest personality calculator can keep up with. This radically undermines young people's ability to experience self-efficacy, giving rise to anxiety and even panic. *While it might theoretically be possible to determine (or even calculate) the course of study that is right for you, you are incapable of doing so.* This situation obviously stands in marked contradiction to the idea articulated above that one needs to be able to allow oneself to be "called," not in order to find the right path in responding to said call, but in order to forge it oneself. Developing such an orientation toward resonance is particularly difficult for high school graduates, who feel that they are standing at a critical crossroads in life where one wrong turn could "screw up everything" that they and their parents built over many years. "My parents have done so much for me and invested so much in me," they think, "and I feel like a total failure because I don't know where I should go."[9] Meanwhile, life experience teaches us that the path our career will take is something that is simply beyond our control or, at best, only semicontrollable. It is absolutely the exception (although we tend to think of it as the "norm") when a person actually ends up becoming what she said she wanted to be in high school. Our career paths are forged in a constant interplay of *listening and responding* both to our internal dispositions and to external circumstances—the opportunities and demands that exist at a given moment—in which process both sides constantly change. Chance and coincidence play just as large a role here as they do in the other central dimension of our lives: family planning.

Everyone knows that the search for a life partner is dominated by uncontrollabilities. And yet here, too, we make every possible effort to "get a handle" on things. This is doubly difficult in matters of love, where not only the other side eludes our control, but also our own side, that is, *our own desires*. Indeed, even our own sexual orientation is completely *beyond our control*, and it is extremely fortunate that efforts to manipulate people's sexuality through all manner of "therapies" (electric shocks, fasting, etc.) are now considered dubious at best. We have just as little say about whom we fall in love with—although here there are a few narrow corridors of control open to us, particularly by virtue of the fact that our choice of partner is not regulated by our desires alone but is also subject to "rational" considerations. Here again, however, new uncontrollabilities emerge from the complex interplay between controllable (rational) and uncontrollable (emotional) elements. Woody Allen illustrates this brilliantly in his 1977 short story "The Lunatic's Tale," in which a surgeon succeeds in transplanting the brain—and thus the intellectual and emotional capacities—of his girlfriend, whom he does not desire physically, into the extremely attractive body of a photographer's model, so as to unite his intellectual and sexual desires in a single person—with the result that he soon falls in love with a third woman who does not seem to conform to either his intellectual or his sexual preferences.[10] Desire, the story seems to suggest, is doubly uncontrollable, a theme to which I will return at the end of this book.

The "practice" of falling in love thus corresponds to the criteria of a resonant event in almost pure form: one is affected, one experiences self-efficacy, there is a transformation that "makes the heavens sing," and both the occurrence and the result are uncontrollable. Thus falling in love is not compatible with a late modern culture geared toward making life controllable. The affected subjects may then realize, with surprise or resignation, that *this relationship*—or even *a relationship—somehow doesn't fit into my life plan.* Nevertheless, they do everything they can to make said relationship fit in, to make it controllable. Meanwhile, ritual and legal ceremonies such as engagement and marriage or, alternatively, attaching a lock to the railing of a bridge or publishing one's relationship status on Facebook help to secure the controllability of our romantic relationships.

The social and legal institution of marriage sets a kind of institutional limit on the uncontrollability of love, one intended to guarantee that both partners are available to, and in a way can be controlled by, each other, even if, as Elisabeth von Thadden points out, this form of control has heretofore been thoroughly defined by patriarchy and gender inequality. As late as 1966, the Fourth Civil Senate of the Federal Court of Justice in Germany ruled that married women had to submit to their husbands physically and serve them, so to speak, with pleasure, or at least *feign* pleasure, even if they did not feel any desire themselves.[11] Hence, if at times marriage has also been referred to or conceived of as the *death of love*, the deeper reason for this seeming paradox lies in the fact that, as I have sought to show, attempting to ensure control over things only robs them of their resonant quality.

If love can be said to constitute one of the major battle lines of the past several centuries, then dating apps like Tinder—which allegedly connects more than 26 million potential couples with each other worldwide every day—represent a new theater in the basic conflict of modernity. Tinder has implemented complex algorithms for finding highly compatible partners ("matches"), some of whom are also presented as "picks," in other words possible matches who conform to an individual's search criteria and click preferences. A date only comes about when both potential partners signal interest in each other by swiping right on the screen. This increases the likelihood of *mutual* attraction while lowering the risk of unrequited desire. Here too we can see the cultural battle between theoretical controllability and practical affirmation of the uncontrollable playing out.

Only a Sideshow? The Digitalization of Our Relationship to the World

The conflict between the two basic orientations of modern life rages not only at the major crossroads of modern life (birth, high school graduation, marriage, etc.), but also along its side streets, in minor activities from daily exercise routines to vacation planning. The technologies and processes associated with digitalization have fundamentally transformed our lives by making nearly the entire world, as it is represented in our consciousness, accessible and controllable in historically unprecedented ways. This world is perceived as only ever being one or two clicks away. It seems to be part of human life in general, or at least of modern human life, that we are confronted with a constant stream of always new questions about the world. When does the train leave again? How late is the supermarket open today? What is the phone number of the personnel office? What's the weather going to be like tomorrow? When was Adenauer chancellor? How did Bayern-Munich do yesterday? What were the results of the French election? Up until about thirty years ago, the answers to such questions were theoretically accessible, but gathering all of them together required hours of work. Today, thank Google, the segments of world in question are all accessible—in the sense of the first dimension of controllability—in a matter of seconds. Knowledge about the world can now be accessed via

search engines and smartphones that we carry constantly on our person, in our pants or jacket pocket. The
change in our relationship to the world associated with
this phenomenon not only affects how subjects relate to
the world (the former now having vast segments of the
latter constantly at their disposal), but also runs in the
opposite direction. In the digital age, the self is also at
the disposal of "the world" in historically unprecedented
ways, not only in the sense of always being reachable via
e-mail and direct messages but also with respect to digi-
tally accessible images, data, and information.

The situation is no different in the consumer world.
Assuming sufficient economic resources, more or less
every product imaginable can be acquired, literally with
a click. In a matter of seconds, the world of commodities, in all its variety, comes into our purview (first and
second dimensions of control) and, through purchasing,
is placed at our disposal (third and fourth dimensions).
It is not only knowledge and commodities that are just
a click away. With the press of a key, we can contact
all our loved and less than loved ones; in a way, we
carry them on our person, too. Without question,
within a very short time, digitalization has radically
revolutionized the relation between controllability and
uncontrollability.

In many respects, the limits of control are no longer
defined by the resistance of the world, but only by the
capacities of our attention spans and wallets. It is not
the world that eludes us or closes itself off from us.
Rather we ourselves are what prevents us from expanding our reach, from increasing our share of the world.
Hence it is no surprise that we ourselves have become
perhaps the most important point of aggression in the

modern relationship to the world. If we want to expand the limits of controllability, we must begin here—and we do, through a variety of self-optimization practices, the most radical form of which we encounter in the "quantified self" movement, the aim of which is to quantify and thus control more or less every aspect of our lives: our blood pressure, our heart rate, the number of steps we take, our blood sugar, caloric intake and calories burned, sleep phases and rest periods, along with their quality, melatonin and serotonin levels, and so on. This is particularly instructive in examining the quasi-intrinsic relation between the various dimensions of controllability. It is all but impossible to keep track of the number of steps one takes in a day without being tempted to increase or optimize that number. It is an illusion to believe that we will not be seduced into changing our behavior by such data, once we have access to them. With their help, we can effectively reduce and sometimes even eradicate the resistance we encounter in the world, including from our own body. *Pain? Shut it out. The fatigue that comes with jetlag? Can be neutralized. Lack of motivation? Can be overcome.* Our relationship to our own bodily processes and psychophysical states has thus been transformed, behind our backs and, in a way, "naturally," from one of flexible, self-efficacious listening and responding to one of technological and medical calculation and control.[12]

Yet does not precisely this open up some space for resonant encounters with the uncontrollable, which actually moves us and which the world has to offer in unlimited abundance? This is exactly what we are looking for, for example, when we travel. Vacation has become a critical mental and libidinal "anchor point" of everyday life for many modern subjects, who think constantly about where their next trip should take them and which segments of world it should "reveal" to them in what ways. Tourism derives its meaning and importance primarily from the fact that we necessarily live our normal professional and family lives in a mode of desperation at the prospect of managing our everyday affairs. As I have sought to show, this consists in a perpetual struggle against our own to-do lists, which we can never completely work through and which, for precisely this reason, have come to epitomize a world consisting of points of aggression that leave us no time, space, or breath for resonant encounters. Thus what vacation promises us is the ability to actually encounter an accommodating world in which there are no tasks we need to accomplish or problems we need to deal with —we can simply let ourselves be genuinely moved. The only problem is that, given the limited time at our disposal and the high costs involved, not only in paying for the trip itself but in living our everyday lives, we expect this experience to be both guaranteed and as intense as possible. As a result, we along with the purveyors of resonance have to use all available means to try to ensure that resonance actually occurs. What is fundamentally uncontrollable should—nay, must—be made available as a commodity, ideally in the form of an "all-inclusive package" that precludes from the outset any possibility of injury or unwelcome self-transformation. By no means do we want to be so affected by Cuba, or Thailand, or the Himalayas that we decide to stay there and give up our job, or lose a fortune, or fall ill, or get mugged. All this should be out of the question. The goal of the vacationer is to return from his or her trip not unpredictably transformed, or possibly even unsettled, but relaxed and reinvigorated. Hence it is no surprise that the cruise industry—which promises travelers that they will encounter faraway lands and people under completely controllable conditions, without having to actually engage with them—is booming. As I have already explained, however, making oneself invulnerable in this way means becoming or remaining incapable of resonance. One might well be stimulated, but certainly not touched or moved. And so here, too, commodity capitalism fulfills its wondrous function of getting consumers to constantly buy new products (in this case, *trips*) only to be inevitably disappointed by them, not so badly that they refrain from purchasing (in principle always identical) commodities altogether, but in such a way that after each disappointment they buy newer and "better" ones.

In my view, tourism in all its variations fulfills a critical function for modern society, not so much—or not only—because it represents an important economic sector, but primarily because it symbolizes, promises, and gives expression to a specific way of relating to the world. For those who visit a travel agency or a website, in a way, the whole world lies at their feet. Turkey, Egypt, even the Seychelles and Easter Island—all are accessible via budget airlines at bargain basement prices, not to everyone, but to those who can afford it, of whom there are many in wealthy industrialized nations. For everyone else, attaining such a relationship to the world remains a goal. The explosive expansion of our share of the world in late modernity is revealed here in vivid detail.

Meanwhile, even in the context of the tourism

industry, or especially there, more and more people, particularly those in the upper middle classes, are beginning to realize that they are at risk of overextending their reach, that the limits of controllability lie not outside but within them, and that precisely this is what they should be working on. As a result, travel packages that temporarily artificially limit our share of the world—those parts of it we can control—have grown increasingly attractive. Spending one's vacation within the walls of a monastery, with no television or internet, or at a solitary mountain cabin, off the grid and without a car, or hiking on foot along the Camino de Santiago or through the Alps from Munich to Venice: here the fact that the segment of world practically available to us has suddenly become much smaller is perceived and experienced as an *unheard-of luxury*. Interestingly, with such offerings, late modernity has managed to make even the experience of extreme uncontrollability controllable, available as a temporary option that we can opt out of at any time.

Aging and Elder Care

In spite of all our efforts, our own age and the process of aging still remain beyond our control. Transhumanists may claim that aging is a treatable illness that can be beaten. Anti-wrinkle creams and anti-aging programs may promise an eternally youthful appearance and inexhaustible vitality. And worldwide, especially in wealthy countries, life expectancy may well have increased by several decades on average—by over thirty years, more than a third of a lifetime—such that here, too, we can speak of a massive temporal expansion of our share of the world. Nevertheless, processes of bodily decay, the finitude of life, represent the hardest limit to modernity's program of increasing our share of the world. All our efforts founder on this ultimate point of aggression.

There is much to be said about late modernity's relationship to illness and disease in general. As Giovanni Maio has convincingly shown, we tend to view illness as something that *we must be able to get a handle on*, that we must be able to avoid by adopting a healthy diet, exercising regularly, getting enough sleep, and so on, or that we must be able to conquer and eliminate through medicine. Modernity's relationship to illness is one of pure aggression—*be gone with it!*—and, when we are unable to beat it, we see ourselves as impotent *failures*. As Maio writes, "[t]he more technology is developed and the more medicine treats illness solely as something catastrophic to be battled against rather than coped with, then the more patients are plunged into despair, the more living with illness becomes an impossible idea."[13] The alternative Maio suggests is precisely what I have sought to describe here as an attitude of *listening and responding*, an attitude that views illness as a kind of "fate" and ascribes to it an audible voice that we must respond to in the way we live our lives:

> The factuality of this world is by no means determinative. A person's fate can instead be seen as an initial starting point from which they can realize their potential by responding to it in their own way. Our fate does not dictate everything. [. . .] What matters is the mindset, the basic attitude with which we respond to what has befallen us. [. . .] Illness, when it is no longer remediable, creates an opportunity for us to react to it in a way that reflects our own personality.[14]

Illness itself remains beyond our control regardless of our "mindset," but the forms of uncontrollability that ailing people face differ. Not least, there is the difference between feeling powerless and experiencing self-efficacy. Paradoxically, the power to make something controllable once again seems to give rise to a feeling of impotence in our subjective relationship to the world.

As far as modern medicine is concerned, it does not really matter who is the patient and who the doctor. The encounter between the two plays no more of a role than does the "encounter" between patient and illness. Symptoms and reactions are quantified, visualized on monitors, targeted, and treated accordingly, and it comes as no surprise that an "optimal treatment," that is, a medical intervention precisely calibrated to the patient's symptoms and condition, either already exists or is expected in the near future, more likely from computerized programs than from human doctors.

The situation is not much different in the field of caretaking, which is inextricably linked with illness, aging, and death. Alfons Maurer recently reflected on the use of digital technologies in elder care as part of a study testing the practical applicability of the concept of resonance, and he offers comprehensive empirical evidence of precisely what I am aiming at in my critique of modernity's control-oriented grasp of the world.[15] Maurer notes that caretakers report a progressive shift in the focus of their attention. In most cases, the interaction between caretaker and patient is no longer an encounter between two unique individuals who "speak with their own voice" each. Instead, the focus is on an ever-growing number of measurable, documentable, and above all optimizable parameters. *How is the patient's blood pressure? Their pulse? Their dosage of medication? What services are needed, and how long will it take to perform them? What sort of insurance benefits are they entitled to? What kind of services can or should be billed? What qualifications do trained assistants need to perform what services? What parameters need to be recorded on what forms?* Doctors and caretakers have to deal with documents, measurements, and display screens under constant time pressures; they are always trying to optimize their performance economically, technologically, medically, and temporally. Meanwhile patients expect the "optimal care" promised them; *who* their caretaker is doesn't matter, so long as the services rendered are parametrically optimized in every respect. There is no longer any space, even at a conceptual level, for caretakers with an individual voice that cannot be made controllable. Digital processes neither produce nor enforce this logic of control, but only *encourage* and *facilitate* it. As Maurer writes, technology could also be implemented differently, namely in a way that is sensitive to resonance—although, in my view, technology cannot itself be sensitive to resonance, or at least is not *capable* of resonance. A future in which parametrically optimized caretaking is performed by robots is eminently conceivable. What would then be lacking is an encounter between two independent, autonomous voices capable of resonance. Studies out of Japan that repeatedly show how happy and grateful patients are with the use of robotic caretakers there appear to undermine this interpretation only at first glance. In my view, these findings demonstrate not that the sick or elderly neither expect nor receive resonance from said robots, but rather that, with the robots' help, they are released from an alienating situation that is severely awkward and uncomfortable for them. In a culture in which bodily processes and odors are perceived as something extremely embarrassing that should be concealed at all costs, and in which it is considered immoral to be a burden to others, requiring any sort of care represents an existentially alienating experience. Robots' performance of the necessary tasks in this situation in place of human beings may not yield any resonant encounters, but it does render merely indifferent what was previously an outright repulsive relationship to the world.

Death

Late modern subjects, like premodern and early modern human beings before them, encounter radical uncontrollability, along with the definitive end of their share in the world, in the fact of death. Both the beginning and the end of life are uncontrollable, even if we can of course violently bring about our own death or that of another person. We do not know when death will come, or how it will come, or what it will be like, or what, if anything, will come after it. Death itself remains fundamentally, categorically, and existentially beyond our control, even if we can and indeed must acknowledge the fact of our own mortality. Hence it is an interesting question whether we can conceive of a resonant relationship with death. Can we listen to death? Can we respond to it? I am inclined to say no, first, because we cannot hear death's "voice" and, second, because self-efficacy in the face of death is an impossibility. We presumably can, however, listen and respond to the fact of our own mortality, as this means listening and responding *to life and the feeling of being alive.* But instead, modern efforts are aimed at making *the process of dying* controllable. Today, Giovanni Maio laments, dying is increasingly understood as a task to be managed and arranged. "We forget that the basic attitude of wanting to do something is particularly ill-suited to coping with dying, of all things. Dying means precisely that life escapes our grasp, hence demanding to have everything under control even as we are dying is in a way inherently contradictory."[16]

The only way to obtain full control over one's own death is to commit suicide. In this premeditated act, we in fact exert authoritative control over life itself, even if only *ex negativo*, by destroying it. The growing practice of *assisted death* likewise makes the end of life semi-controllable, subject to the will of the dying person, if only under limited conditions. Both suicide and assisted dying exhibit aspects of a self-efficacious action that can also be understood as a responsive act. At the same time, we see manifested here the modern rejection of the idea that there is anything beyond the control of the subject, that there is any limit to our control beyond what is technically possible. In both cases, dying appears as a point of aggression, a task to be mastered.

Beyond this, we also seek to maintain control over the last phase of our life before we die, even in the event that we are no longer able to consciously exercise this control ourselves, via all manner of *advanced healthcare directives*, which specify what forms of treatment should be administered to us, who will be entitled to make such decisions, what should be done with our organs and our bodies after we die, and so on. Questions surrounding testaments and inheritance arrangements are of particular interest in this context, as these allow us to exercise a form of control over our property and "legacy" beyond our own death. Our last will defines the segments of world we still have control over even after we, the bearer of said will, have died. Wills and testaments allow us to cheat death in a way, insofar as they temporally extend our reach beyond the end of our own life. On the way to death, however, life continues to exhibit its fundamental uncontrollability with all force and clarity. People who, while they are still alive, attempt to use their last will and testament, along with various forms of inheritance or transfer, as a way of being prepared for all the vagaries and vicissitudes of old age—*What if I die before my spouse? What if he or she dies before me? What if my new daughter-in-law turns against me? What if I require long-term care? What if my son wants to sell the house? What if my grandchildren reach out, or I meet a new life partner, or a fight breaks out between my children, or my daughter loses her job and can no longer pay her credit card bills?* and so on—generally tend only to make themselves and their loved ones miserable. The existential uncontrollabilities of life not only remain unpredictable, they become more unpredictable than ever and certainly cannot be brought under control in a notarized document. Listening and responding to the vagaries and vicissitudes of life as they arise, by contrast, seems to be a much more promising strategy.

7

Control as an Institutional Necessity

The Structural Dimension of the Basic Conflict of Modernity

In the last chapter I described the tense relationship between our desire to take firm control of various segments of world and our longing to enter into a resonant, responsive relationship with them, or *with life itself*, in the form of individual life choices. In this chapter I would like to turn to the sociostructural side of things and examine the ways in which the basic conflict of modernity has been institutionalized in different social spheres. My core thesis is that the mode of dynamic stabilization characteristic of modern society structurally imposes the constant expansion of our share of the world and thereby enforces a program of making the world limitlessly controllable, thus codifying the aggressive relationship to the world that I identified in Chapter 1. But the fact that the world nevertheless continues to elude us, repeatedly proving itself to be *uncontrollable* in spite of all our efforts, is itself a functional requirement without which social life would long since have become rigid and sclerotic. In consequence, the dynamism of social life is generated precisely by the constantly shifting frontlines in the conflict between what is controllable and what is uncontrollable. But how specifically does this happen? I would like to pursue this question through recourse to five basic trends in modern social life.

"We Can't Afford It": The Compulsion to Optimize

The structural dimension of the basic conflict of modernity manifests itself in the fact that a society capable only of dynamic stabilization *cannot accept uncontrollability*, even though it *requires* it everywhere. The compulsion toward continual escalation inherent in the logics of growth, acceleration, and innovation implies that efficiency and output, or process and result, must constantly be optimized at every level. By contrast, the element of uncontrollability characteristic of resonant relationships requires engaging in processes the very occurrence of which is uncertain and the outcomes of which remain open-ended. In other words, we do not know whether resonance will even happen, and still less what will result from it. This is something no private company or public agency can afford. Optimization means achieving the best possible result in the shortest possible time, while maintaining constant control over the processes involved. The basic modes of process control—in the economy, in politics, in caretaking, in education, and so on—are calculation and mastery. Strictly speaking, time and cost pressures alone suffice to clarify the problem. Someone who needs to get to the airport immediately has no time for any conversation, idea, landscape, music, or person that may cross his path, lest he miss his flight. A person who wants to pass a test likewise must not allow herself to be "reachable" to anything or anyone. She can brook no distractions and must not get involved in any activities the content or length of which is uncertain. Nurses and caretakers, who need to account for their actions minute by minute, cannot allow themselves any open-ended interactions with their patients, while universities cannot offer a course of study without making clear how long it takes to complete the program and what skills will be acquired in the process. Health insurance plans cannot cover treatments the duration and success of which are uncertain (as psychoanalytic therapists know all too well), and no one wants to fund an open-ended research program. *The output must add up and must be predictable and manageable in terms of both time and content.* This is what the institutional logic of dynamic stabilization demands.

Upon closer inspection, however, in all institutional spheres of operation, uncontrollabilities are, surprisingly, not only unavoidable but practically indispensable. Every teacher knows that the most formative educational processes occur outside the curriculum, and often precisely in those moments when the curriculum —which seeks to codify what students need to learn and master when—plays no role whatsoever. Every director of a research and development department understands that real innovations, "disruptive," pathbreaking discoveries cannot be engineered or predicted. Every doctor is aware that, at least in cases of serious illness, healing and recovery depend on uncontrollable individual factors. The entertainment industry likewise operates on the knowledge that market success cannot be engineered, not with money and not with technology. A book, a film, or a song can be considered and rejected by every major publisher, studio, or label and still become a worldwide hit. Or, conversely, it may well flop despite a multimillion-dollar advertising campaign. And, as discussed in the introduction, sports —particularly professional soccer—would be utterly uninteresting if success could simply be bought or calculated.

The process of academic research is particularly well suited for illustrating the contradictory complex of problems involved here. A scholar who, say, wants to study the concept of resonance, or uncontrollability, or the possibility of a post-growth economy cannot possibly say in advance whether his research will actually produce anything noteworthy, what he will find, or when he will find it. But, so as not to squander what is often taxpayer money, funding institutions demand precise, formalized research applications that provide detailed information about how a study will be designed, what steps will be taken, what partners and contributors will be involved, what results are expected when, and how and where these results will be published. Scholarship is thus supposed to be made controllable in terms of time, financing, and "output." This is, not least, a political requirement.

The tense relationship between our efforts to manufacture control and the need to accept uncontrollability can also be seen in the political process itself. As a rule, when modern political parties announce a new platform, they have already precisely calculated, through opinion polls and market research, how much support or resistance they can count on, for which ideas, from what population groups. To their surprise, however, the ensuing public debate always goes differently from expected and develops its own, uncontrollable dynamic —a necessity if we are even to be able to speak of a political process at all. It is the uncontrollability of politics that in turn angers voters, who may then seek to force their representatives to be politically predictable and manageable through "imperative mandates" and popular referenda.

Anyone who reads the news attentively knows that what comes out of any attempt to implement a political program truly is uncontrollable[1]—even as political campaigns are waged almost exclusively with promises of enhancement and improvement, in other words with promises that the future can be engineered. Yet policies aimed at creating more jobs, higher pensions, better environmental conditions, more affordable housing, more efficient public transportation, more peaceful international relations, and so on not infrequently achieve the opposite of what they promise. The dynamism of sociopolitical life arises precisely from the fact that the latter is not engineerable.

"People Would Take Advantage": The Logic of Bureaucracy and the Demand for Justice

It is not only the logic of dynamic stabilization or the compulsion toward economic growth that demands predictability and control, reducing our tolerance for the uncontrollable. The ethically and politically well-founded principles of justice and equal treatment similarly demand the systematic elimination of all forms of *arbitrariness* and undue advantage. As Max Weber argues in his writings on bureaucracy,[2] these principles form the basic operative ethical and legal framework of modern public policy and administration. They make the political and social world calculable and manageable for actors such as entrepreneurs and investors, as well as for planners and consumers. They make social life *dependable*. Indeed, it would appear blatantly unjust if public authorities began invoking "uncontrollability" as a reason to treat individuals or institutions *differently* when it comes to, say, awarding building contracts, determining employment qualifications, issuing permits, or evaluating performance. In all these situations, we expect not only equal treatment but also fair assessment, on the basis of codified standards that are reasonable and predictable.

A network of legal and administrative regulations endeavor to make all the vagaries and vicissitudes of life a priori controllable in this way. It must be clear which rules apply when, where, and to whom. Uncontrollability, however, proves to be a stubborn, Janus-faced adversary. The dictates of equal treatment yield manifest injustice again and again, because life cannot be made controllable. The choice is frequently one between Scylla and Charybdis. Establishing strict rules and regulations designed to ensure that no one can abuse basic government benefits, for example, inevitably produces cases of unintended but cruel hardship: *the elderly woman at the pharmacy who can no longer afford her medication, the child who cannot go on the class trip, the father who has to draw from his daughter's savings account*, and so on. Conversely, attempting to avoid creating such hardships means accepting that aid will be disbursed in many cases where it appears unjustified. Trying to prevent both circumstances requires formulating endlessly complex sets of rules and regulations—and still failing to achieve the desired goal. The situation is the same (if not even more ambivalent) with respect to the question of when and whether countries should grant asylum and to whom. How can we evaluate and compare people's circumstances and living conditions in their native countries? The conclusion that actually emerges is that—legally, administratively, and politically—we should not ignore the fact that there are things we cannot control, but instead we should find ways of dealing with them.

For, as a result of our efforts to make social life legally and bureaucratically controllable in ever more comprehensive ways, in many areas of life, the uncontrollable dynamism of social processes has been not only radically restrained, but brought to a total standstill. Legal determinations, process controls, and procedural regulations have spread like a blight across what ought to be a vibrantly evolving social life. At a recent conference devoted to the question of how cities can become spaces of resonance for their citizens, the mayor of a large German city reported that, at youth centers and youth assemblies, most people's eyes "light up" when ideas are presented to establish new public spaces, schools, or festivals. Unfortunately, however, he always has to pump the brakes: *Nice idea, but this proposal, that approval, these legal assessments, and those permits and safeguards are all required before it can be implemented.* And, with this, all the energy in the room "fizzles out." Here we can experience, directly and even physically, the birth of severe "alienation" as a result of encountering a non-responsive, indifferent, or repulsive social world. Almost everyone who has ever had a "nice idea" has had such an experience, whether at a summer camp, in the workplace, at a care facility, working with refugees, or even in one's community orchestra or local athletic club, where things not infrequently run smoothly and productively only and precisely when the usual rules and responsibilities are ignored.

"And Whose Responsibility Is This?" The Demand for Transparency and Documentation

Ignoring rules and regulations, however, is not only risky, but—in a world geared toward controllability and optimization—increasingly difficult, as controllability also means accountability. Once again: we have to deal with uncontrollabilities in all social processes, wherever social life happens. (All sorts of secure processes may occur in mechanical or bureaucratic contexts where everything can in fact be calculated and controlled—but no social life is to be found here.) Hence a society that, in all these processes and in the face of all uncontrollabilities that accompany them, is structurally compelled to constantly ask, "Who is responsible for this? Who bears the costs?" will systematically run into difficulties. We witness such problems in schools, government agencies, private companies, care facilities, grocery stores, social clubs, and so on—in any place where designated officials (fire prevention officers, first aiders, equal opportunity representatives, youth protection officers, workplace health officers, and so on) are authorized to handle every conceivable occurrence, for which they are trained and prepared and armed with comprehensive informational materials, and where records and documentation have to be produced about everything.

Today nearly all employees and professionals—not only, but particularly in what is called "social" professions—complain that they are scarcely able to get around to their actual work or no longer have time to do it well. This is by no means solely a result of the modern compulsion toward economic growth and acceleration; it is also precisely because of their or their employers' futile efforts to make all processes and conditions in the workplace fully transparent (dimension 1 of controllability), attributable (dimension 2), manageable (dimension 3), and efficient (dimension 4). Teachers and professors feel that they hardly have any time for their students; doctors, that they have no time to dedicate to their patients. Scholars are unable to get around to their research; caretakers, to caring for their patients; auto mechanics, to actually repairing people's cars. In job after job, people are increasingly occupied with writing, examining, and assessing ever longer reports, proposals, and other documents. The blight of having to make everything controllable has everywhere infected the uncontrollable productivity of social life.

The desire to establish responsibility and accountability exhibits other problematic characteristics as well. We seek out guilty or responsible parties wherever accidents and misfortunes occur, on the assumption that the conditions that produced them were "essentially" controllable. *Someone must be responsible for this.* The tragic events at the 2010 Love Parade in Duisburg, where more than twenty people lost their lives and over five hundred were seriously injured as a result of a mass panic, offer a possible example of this. Sixteen investigations were subsequently opened to determine whether any errors were committed with respect to planning and regulating the influx of parade goers. *Someone must be to blame. Somebody has to be brought to account.* I cannot and do not want to judge whether or not grievous mistakes were made in this instance. I merely wish to point out that there was and is simply no space in public and political discourse for the idea —the reality—of uncontrollability in social life. This is why we reflexively seek out "responsible parties" even in the event of natural disasters such as earthquakes and floods. Someone *must* have violated building regulations, disregarded safety precautions, ignored warning signs. Again and again, all our political and discursive energy seems to coalesce into outrage directed against those who failed to prepare for or subsequently manage the disaster in question. It is of course difficult to accept that *essentially avoidable* accidents happen—that, for example, children sometimes die on the playground or while playing sports, even when this could have been prevented. But it is time that we began to comprehend what price we pay for trying to eliminate this possibility more and more radically and categorically, to make it essentially unthinkable.

"I Paid for It, I'm Entitled to It": Commodification and Legalism

We encounter efforts to make the fundamentally uncontrollable controllable not only on the work–production side of things, but also on the consumer side. The commodification of nearly every aspect of our relationship to the world—the fact that nearly every object and process is on offer in late modern society as a service or as a commodity—implies a *legal right to controllability*.

Purchasing something fundamentally means being able to control it, having it at one's disposal; controllability lies at the heart of the concept of property.[3] Hence quality assurance is of critical interest to both producers and consumers: a purchased product must possess all qualities and components implicitly or explicitly included in the sales agreement (and no others . . .).

The matter of the relation between controllability and uncontrollability becomes particularly interesting when it comes to the purchase of non-material things. What exactly are we entitled to when we buy an expensive concert or theater ticket? *That the performers be punctual, in a good mood, and inspired? That the performance be free of any noisy disruptions? That it last at least ninety minutes?* What can we demand when we book a vacation? *That the weather be good, the other guests healthy and polite, the street quiet, the food tasty?* What must concert performers and travel service providers, to take just these two examples, be able to rule out? What are they responsible for? Bumper-to-bumper highway traffic? Missed or delayed flights? Flash floods? Steady rains? Ants on the terrace? Snapped guitar strings? Collapsed drum risers? The countless lawsuits filed year after year regarding these and similar occurrences make it clear just how much demand for comprehensive controllability has risen on the side of consumers and consumer protection—a trend driven in no small part by the fact that the purveyors of such services constantly imply, promise, and above all *sell* controllability. In many respects, however, this ultimately amounts to a kind of helpless shadow-boxing, as the core promise of the services provided—feeling relaxed and transformed on vacation, being moved and inspired by a concert, in short, *experiencing resonance* —ultimately is and remains uncontrollable, precisely because it *cannot be commodified*. Whether at a concert or on vacation, taking a dance class or receiving a massage, a person who is focused or insists on getting absolutely everything she feels entitled to, everything she was promised would be at her disposal, will most likely miss out on the uncontrollable experience that was the reason why she decided to engage in the activity in the first place.

"You Touch Them, and They Stultify/You Are the Very Destroyer of Things": Identity Thinking as a Basic Operating Principle

These reflections, once again, make it clear that the demand for comprehensive controllability and, with it, the fundamental contradiction at the heart of modernity, have become both institutionalized and habituated, permeating our social institutions and practices just as they shape our own inner attitude. What I identified at the beginning of this essay as the modern *attitude of aggression* defines our relationship to the world in every aspect of our existence, down to our "conceptual control" over the world. Uncontrollability has become an intellectual impossibility, because we conceive of it only as that which is not yet controllable or that which we have yet to bring under our control,[4] and therefore also an experiential impossibility, because we cannot develop any responsive relationship to it, only one of powerlessness against it. What Theodor W. Adorno pejoratively called "identity thinking" has become totalitarian.[5] Identity thinking can be understood as the idea that one has grasped the essence of a thing, an event, or a process and, by conceptualizing it, made it intellectually controllable. But this overlooks the fact that there is always a gap, a rift between the subject and the world or the other that the subject seeks to comprehend, and that it is only in this gap, in what eludes us and remains beyond our grasp, that true, vibrant experience shines forth. Thus, for Adorno, the compulsion to make the entire world controllable and to cut out that which cannot be controlled begins with *thinking itself*—not with the content of thought, but with our way of thinking, our intellectual attitude—and thus is embedded in our innermost perception of the world.

The poet Rainer Maria Rilke, writing nearly seventy years before Adorno but just as pointedly and vividly, gets to the heart of this critique of humanity's reifying, downright *mortifying* linguistic and intellectual grip on the world in one of his famous "thing poems," which reads as follows:

> I am so afraid of people's words.
> Everything they pronounce is so clear:
> this is a hand, and that is a house,
> and beginning is here, and the end over there.
>
> Their meaning frightens, their mockery-play
> and their claims to know what's coming, what was;
> no mountain thrills them now; their estates
> and their gardens abut directly on God.
>
> I warn; I ward them off. Stay back.
> It's a wonder to me to hear things sing.
> You touch them, and they stultify.
> You are the very destroyer of things.[6]

Following Rilke's poem, the blight that has infected social life through a web of bureaucratic regulations and our constant compulsion to optimize has its origins in modernity's intellectual and linguistic grasp of the world. Igor Levit says that he never wants to be "finished" with anything. Identity thinking operates according to the opposite principle: it is always already finished with everything. This is easily and clearly illustrated through everyday situations. Let us imagine that we are captivated by the sight of the moon, turn to our companion, and say: *Oh, look, the moon!* To which they respond: *What about it? It's been there the whole time. It's just a rocky orb, 385,000 kilometers away, littered with craters, without any life. It's been like that for millions of years, it never changes. What are you talking about?* We wouldn't know what to say. That is in fact what the moon is. But it is not only that. It is also an object of fear and desire and longing, and has been for millennia. It's the moon of "Fly Me to the Moon," *Dark Side of the Moon*, and thousands of other songs and fairy tales. Its biological significance as well as its psychological influence on us are still not entirely clear scientifically. It even has an important social meaning, as it structures and modifies our social rhythms and calendars. But, in going after all of these different meanings and trying to "nail them down," we too are already in the realm of fixating, mortifying identity thinking, *the very destroyer of things*. It is impossible to enter into a responsive relationship with the moon in this way; nor can we explain in this way what we meant when we called out to our companion, "Look!"

Meanwhile, astrophysicists along with micro- and particle physicists tell us that there is something not right with our human perception of time, space, and causality, our distinction between observing subject and observed object—or rather that our basic concepts of reality, of *what there is*, are utterly unstable and tenuous.[7] With respect to the smallest particles of matter, we cannot even say any more that they exist, only that they *tend to exist*. One need not be an esoteric or cosmic kook to assert that we are nowhere close to being "finished" with what reality is—not conceptually, and certainly not in terms of our relationship with it.

Identity thinking robs us of the possibility of relating to what we encounter as an uncontrollable other, whom we would first have to listen to before we could respond to it. We encounter objects instead as things to be known, paid for, acquired, managed, and mastered, and for each of these aggressive relationships there is now a corresponding app. We experience things as being essentially controllable in all these respects, even when they elude our actual control, when we do *not* know, possess, or command them. According to Adorno and Rilke, however, this means that we do not experience the full phenomenological complexity of things, but only those aspects of them that we have made controllable conceptually, economically, and technologically.

We are never finished with the world we encounter, although we frequently and increasingly encounter it as though we were: *this is a hand, and that is a house.* This extends even to these reflections on uncontrollability. Indeed, it is not always easy for me to explain what this essay is actually about. *What are you writing a book about? About the fact that we don't have a handle on everything? That we can control some things and not others? That sometimes chance is determinative?*

Control as an Institutional Necessity

That's always been the case, it still is, and it probably always will be. What are you going to write about that?! Having arrived at this difficult juncture of writing or speaking, it can be helpful to go back and reflect once again on the nature of desire.

8

The Uncontrollability of Desire and the Desire for the Uncontrollable

It should be clear even to the most stringent economic, bureaucratic, or conceptual reifier that we have no control over our own desires—and at the same time that the structure, direction, and objects of this desire are not simply a matter of chance. As we saw through the example of Woody Allen's "The Lunatic's Tale," we cannot command our libido. Whom we erotically or sexually desire, what arouses or attracts us is something beyond our own volition. Likewise, our taste in food and drink, music and literature, clothing and fashion, where and how we want to live, along with our wants, our longings, our sympathies and antipathies are to a large extent simply "given" to us. If modernity is geared toward making the world controllable, this arrangement is rooted primarily in our desire to make it available for our libido. Yet, in our actions and in what we might call our life choices, we nevertheless find that we are not simply driven and defined by our desires or appetites. It is rather the case that we attempt to *respond* to our desires by how we live our lives. We develop our wants and convictions in constant confrontation with the structure and content of desire, a confrontation in which desire itself is also constantly transformed—although often in unpredictable ways, as Woody Allen shows us. Our relation to desire thus exhibits all the characteristics of a resonant relationship in almost pure form. It is, always, directly in play whenever we find ourselves called or we allow ourselves to be affected by something. We respond to it physically, mentally, and emotionally. We are transformed by it, and at the same time the structure of our desire itself constantly shifts and changes. In the process, we often naturally experience self-efficacy rather than feeling that we are merely victims of our own appetites—even though we cannot simply control them. Indeed, our situation is not unlike that of Igor Levit with the "Moonlight" Sonata. We repeatedly discover new sides of ourselves, to which we then respond; and, as we get to know ourselves better and learn to understand our own reactions to things, we may deepen our skills and expertise, but we are never "finished" with ourselves. It seems to me critically important, however, that we do not experience or conceive of the uncontrollability at play in our relation to ourselves as mere chance, but as a genuinely *responsive relationship*. Here as in any relationship, incapacity for resonance can assume two contrary forms. If we were to *always give in* to our desires, we would be nothing but pure "voluptuaries" (or "wantons" in the philosopher Harry Frankfurt's sense).[1] We would cease to be sane, accountable subjects and would be incapable of living a life. We would lack our "own voice" with which to respond to our desires. This voice, as Charles Taylor has brilliantly demonstrated in his various works, is formed primarily through "strong evaluations"[2]—our convictions, based on our experience, that there are things in the world that are simply important regardless of whether we desire them or not, indeed even if *we do not desire them*, and especially then. God's commandments, moral law, reason in Kant's sense, international solidarity, the natural world, which we ought to listen to—these are all examples of "things" people orient themselves by and try to abide by, even if they are rather more inclined to act contrary to them. However, if people always and exclusively abide by such ideals and the norms and principles derived from them and *never* give in to their desires—perhaps even because the idea that one ought never to let oneself be guided by one's desires is itself a strong evaluation for them —they become hardened against themselves and the world, and thus incapable of resonance. The result of this is self-alienation: our will, conduct, and conception of ourselves all fall apart, because our own wants (and actions, insofar as we still allow them to be determined by our desires) appear foreign to us.

The uncontrollability of desire is further demonstrated by the fact that we have yet to succeed in creating artificial intelligence or robots capable of *desiring*. In my view, this is scarcely even conceivable. We know by now that robots are capable of being highly creative and innovative, generating patterns and connections never seen before and finding approaches to problem-solving that we would not have arrived at ourselves. But, while we can give them objectives and they are potentially even capable of seeking out their own, they cannot *desire*. A world of artificial intelligence would thus lack the crucial motivating energy that drives a dynamic social life.

The Uncontrollability of Desire

To understand this energy, it is critically important to recognize that desire is itself always directed toward something uncontrollable. We desire what we cannot have—or at least what we cannot have immediately or entirely, or what we cannot completely control. For Igor Levit, the "Moonlight" Sonata is "desirable" only as long as it continues to elude him or confront him as something unfamiliar. A sex doll that we can control in every respect may well be able to give us gratification, but it seems to me that we cannot truly desire it—unless we project uncontrollable characteristics onto it. This is the same principle that binds the libido to all kinds of games. As I explained above, a game is interesting only if we cannot completely control its progression or result. In games as in love, however, uncontrollability does not mean pure contingency or blind chance. We are speaking here of *responsive* relationships, even if in extreme cases—such as when we love someone who is unattainable to us—receiving a response is something we can only dream of.

This in fact seems to me to be inherent in the basic structure of desire: desire is driven by a longing to bring something as yet unreachable within our reach. And precisely this might provide us with a key to depriving modernity's boundless game of escalation—its endeavor to make everything and everyone controllable—of the motivating energy it requires, and to doing so by somehow "unplugging" its connection to our libido. My contention is that the basic structure of human desire is a desire for relationships. We want to reach or bring within reach something that is not "at hand." This something might be a new guitar, a tablet computer, a lake, or someone we love. In all these cases, desire aims at establishing a responsive relationship with its object. But desire is extinguished, I argue, when there is no longer anything to "discover" about our counterpart, when we have mastered or can command every aspect of it, when we have complete control over it. Here again, we can speak of "semicontrollability." We cannot desire a person or a guitar if we know nothing about them or have never seen them. An object of desire must be at least partly or temporarily controllable in the first dimension, otherwise our desire is merely a "nameless longing" that ultimately desires only desire itself. Complete control in all four dimensions, however, extinguishes desire. *Games become meaningless, music loses its appeal, love grows cold.* When it comes to desire, complete uncontrollability is *futile*, complete control *unappealing*. This means that a successful relationship to the world aims not at making things controllable, but at bringing them within reach. Our counterpart must be reachable in some way; we must be able to establish a responsive relationship with them that is neither erratic, and thus completely arbitrary, nor entirely controllable, and that from this very structure sets in motion the interplay between "callability," self-efficacy and transformation, thus allowing us to feel alive.

If my arguments here are sound, then modern culture has committed a fundamental error in transforming our always open-ended longing to bring the world within reach into a demand to bring it reliably under control, a demand that has been systematized into a program of constant expansion of our share of the world, making it controllable in all four dimensions. This confusion of reachability and controllability finds perhaps its most consequential expression in the translation of our fundamental human *desire for relationships* into a *desire for objects*. Unlike relationships, objects can be thoroughly and reliably controlled. The logic of consumerism and commodity capitalism is thus based on responding to our unquenchable longing for resonance in the form of a promise of controllability, which channels the desires that guide our actions toward objects themselves. In effect, this corresponds to a process of fetishization. The qualities we desire—the ability to be "called" and transformed in a way that allows us to experience self-efficacy—are ascribed to objects and commodities (cruises, desert safaris, Ayurveda cures, etc.); we seek fulfillment not through the uncertain, uncontrollable process of adaptive transformation, but through the reliable, controllable appropriation of commodified objects.[3] But having access to and control over purchased products cannot fulfill the tacit promise of resonance. The magic trick that capitalism manages to pull off is thus to leave us as consumers constantly disappointed by the objects we have acquired, not so much that we stop desiring and purchasing them, but in such a way that we insatiably desire ever newer and ever different ones, in an infinitely escalating spiral of hope and disappointment (in which we never actually find what it is we are seeking).[4]

A completely controllable world would be not only unappealing, but without resonance. There would be nothing left in it to desire, desire would have no object, and our fundamental need to find a responsive counterpart would remain unsatisfied. Modernity has given us extraordinary, incomprehensible access to and control over the world. There are ample indications that libido, burning desire, "fiery" longing is on the wane in contemporary society, such that many observers are already speaking of a post-emotional, post-sexual age.[5] At the same time, there are even more indications that frustration and depression are on the rise. This is expressed politically as disappointment in the fact that life has not made good on what it promised us, that modern society has failed to deliver what we hoped for from it. Particularly in the more affluent regions of the late modern world, where economic and technological access to and control over the world has reached unprecedented proportions, enraged citizens (themselves often quite well-off) are taking to the streets and seizing majorities. What are they so angry about? What promises have not been kept? What is at the root of their generalized resentment against the world?

Further psychological, philosophical, and sociological analysis of the structure of human desire and our corresponding anxieties and frustrations, a critique of the ideology of our own desires, could be a promising way out of the labyrinth of a resonanceless, escalation-oriented society, helping us to change how we relate to the world.[6] If we no longer saw the world as a point of aggression, but as a point of resonance that we approach, not with an aim of appropriating, dominating, and *controlling* it but with an attitude of listening and responding, an attitude oriented toward self-efficacious adaptive transformation, toward mutually *responsive reachability*, modernity's escalatory game would become meaningless and, more importantly, would be deprived of the psychological energy that drives it. A different world would become possible. There is another, potentially deeply unattractive world, however, which is not only possible but even likely—and for entirely different reasons, as our efforts to create a controllable world appear to be culminating in the exact opposite, namely in unbridled uncontrollability.

9
The Monstrous Return
of the Uncontrollable

If my observations up to this point have given the impression that the world has become almost limitlessly controllable for late modern subjects, this is, at best, only a half-truth. For the process of making the world controllable also has a serious, paradoxical flipside: in many respects, the late modern lifeworld is becoming increasingly uncontrollable, unpredictable, and uncertain. Uncontrollability has returned in many areas of everyday life, but in a new and frightening form, almost as a self-made monster.

The reason why we are confronted with frustrating, anxiety-inducing uncontrollabilities everywhere in our daily lives lies, first and foremost, in the categorial gulf between theoretical control and actual control, the concurrence of controllability in theory and uncontrollability in practice. Anyone who has ever tried to roll down the windows or release the handbrake on their car when its electrical systems are jammed has experienced this. Minor problems that only a few years ago could be resolved with a few flicks of the wrist or a hammer now require calling a tow truck and ordering expensive replacement parts that could take weeks to arrive. And anyone who has ever found themselves trapped in their own car because the anti-theft lock snapped irrevocably shut, refusing to be circumvented, has experienced first-hand what monstrous forms this new breed of uncontrollability can assume. Things that were firmly in our grasp for centuries are now suddenly totally out of reach. It will suffice to give just a few examples here: locks that cannot be opened, lights and machines that we are unable to turn off, computers that behave completely erratically, televisions that turn on by themselves, e-mails that never arrive or disappear on their own from our inboxes, and so on. And it is not only laypeople who often feel clueless and powerless here. Retailers and repair shops frequently cannot do anything other than exchange malfunctioning parts or send them back to the manufacturer. For them as for consumers, this lack of control generates extreme frustration simply because it severely undermines their expectations of self-efficacy. It is not only the uncontrollability of objects, but our complete inability to even reach them that drives us to despair and into "cold" (and occasionally also hot) fury.

It is not only technological complexity, but also the complexity and speed of social processes that generate uncontrollability, particularly in terms of the shape of the future. Let us look again at the process of choosing a career or a course of study. In contrast to a situation in which one had perhaps only a dozen or two skilled occupations to choose from, each tied to a clear life and career path—apprenticing at a bakery meant becoming a baker, training as a mechanic led to a presumably lifelong career in that field until one retired at 65, and so on—today it is practically impossible even to keep track of all the vocational training programs at our disposal, let alone predict how our professional life might turn out. A predictable career path that we could plan out and at least partly shape ourselves has become an erratic, uncontrollable ride. And, despite the unpredictability and uncontrollability of our circumstances, we are still held responsible for results that we are supposed to have been able to foresee, which gives rise to anxiety. Controllability in theory thus transforms uncontrollability in practice into a menacing "monster," the kind of threat that lurks around every corner but that we can neither see nor control.

Such monsters have also emerged in the course of the "digitalization" of life wherever processes and situations have become increasingly parametrically visible, that is, controllable in the first dimension. We are aware of more and more physiological parameters (body mass index, blood pressure, heart rate, blood sugar, serotonin and melatonin levels, etc.) and are able to influence, if not command, the values that correspond to them. We also have more and more "parametrized" information about the contents of our diet and how different ingredients affect all the metrics mentioned here. This information is highly contradictory and confusing, however, such that more and more people are increasingly uncertain about what and when they should or should not eat. Everyday activities such as cooking and eating—not to mention having and raising children, or even sleeping, walking, heating and ventilating our living spaces, loving and caressing, and so on—which we had a firm handle on for centuries and which were a constant source of experiences of self-efficacy in our relationship to the world, have suddenly become occasions for feeling uncertain, insecure, and powerless. Our own everyday lives and actions seem to be increasingly beyond our control, and not even the experts who appear to be the guardians of "theoretical" controllability are capable of creating even the *impression* of control through calculation. The expansion of our technological reach is not increasing our self-efficacy, but undermining it. We feel ourselves powerless or blameworthy in an unresponsive world. Information about our objective body tells us nothing about the state of our phenomenal body (which is categorically uncontrollable, although highly responsive). These are medical and technological parameters that confront us as external data, with which we have no "inner" perceptual relationship. Our own bodies have become *practically* inaccessible to us. Remarkably, the situation is no different in the macrosphere of politics, through which we collectively shape the world. The expansion of our technological and economic reach, together with the waning of tradition and the rise of pluralism, has made the contemporary social world "controllable"—that is, malleable—to an unprecedented degree. No church, no king or queen, and in many respects not even nature sets any limits on what is available to us, what we can control. And yet, astonishingly, political actors feel (or at least present themselves as being) utterly powerless. From Margaret "There Is No Alternative" Thatcher to Gerhard "Basta!" Schröder, the belief has set in among political leaders that the basic parameters of political action are defined by markets, processes of globalization, and the logic of competition. They themselves have no control over these processes; there is no alternative.

One can only act "wrongly," fall behind in global competition, and thus squander one's opportunities for future control.

Recent trends strongly suggest, however, that this supposed lack of any alternative can be overcome. Things are happening now—Brexit, the reinstitution of torture, mercantilist protectionism in the form of massive tariffs and trade wars—that until very recently were unthinkable, only at the price of global politics becoming completely unpredictable. The political world now seems to resist any dependable configuration or rational planning—as has long been the cases with financial markets. This impression of a world becoming increasingly politically uncontrollable is further reinforced by the similarly uncontrollable dynamism of media and social networks, which have rapidly become capable of provoking previously unimagined, massively consequential waves of outrage or excitement that are unpredictable and uncontrollable in terms of how they arise, how they pass away, and how they interact with one another.

Hence it can come as no surprise that sociological approaches to the social world are increasingly drawing on chaos theory, with the suggestion that there are often no clear links between causes and effects. Sometimes tremendous economic and military efforts (say, to "modernize" and "democratize" Afghanistan) end up being utterly ineffective, while in other cases a tiny, insignificant incident (such as the publication of a cartoon image of Mohammed in a Danish newspaper) can trigger major shifts and worldwide condemnation.[1] If bringing the world under control means making it manageable and predictable, then the political–social world today is becoming increasingly uncontrollable at a breathtaking pace.

In the end, modernity's program of making the world controllable threatens to produce a new, radical form of uncontrollability, one that is categorically different from and worse than the original, because we are incapable of experiencing self-efficacy or of establishing a responsive relationship of adaptive transformation when confronted with it. Nothing symbolizes this paradoxical inversion more spectacularly than the project of nuclear power. With the development of the technological capacity to split atoms and harness the energy released, modernity ascended to a new level of control over matter. With the ability to create radioactive isotopes, it brought the "essence" of matter, its innermost animating principle, within reach, and with it the ability to create new worlds. The optimistic, even utopian expectations of the early atomic age scientists, who measured themselves against the very creation, speak for themselves. "The interior of an exploding fission bomb," Robert Oppenheimer once wrote, "is, so far as we know, a place without parallel elsewhere. It is hotter than the center of the sun; it is filled with matter that does not normally occur in nature [. . .]. In the crudest, simplest sense, it is quite true that in atomic weapons man has created novelty."[2] Today, seven decades after Oppenheimer's euphoria, it no longer needs even to be said that this radical seizure of power over matter produced the most terrible menace known to humanity: the monster of nuclear radiation, which is monstrous in several respects.[3] First, because radioactivity unleashed, as at Chernobyl or Fukushima, ultimately cannot be managed or controlled at all. At best, we can try to "bury" and thus contain it, although we will hardly be able to manage this over the thousands of years that are necessary. Second, radioactivity turns out to be perhaps the most monstrously uncontrollable opponent humanity could confront, because it undermines our self-efficacy more radically than any other threat we know: we cannot even perceive it with our senses. It is silent, invisible, odorless, impalpable. As Martin Repohl has argued, this categorically changes our relationship to the world even where it is not radioactive, as we can no longer tell whether a segment of world—a landscape, a flower, an apple—is harmless and pleasant or toxic and deadly simply by looking at it. It is utterly impossible to establish a resonant relationship with radioactivity. Adaptively transforming it would be lethal; experiencing self-efficacy, impossible.

This brings the core argument of this final chapter into sharp focus. The uncontrollability generated by processes intended to make the world controllable produces a radical alienation. Modernity's program of expanding our reach into a world that it has transformed into an accumulation of points of aggression produces fear of a loss of world and of the world falling mute in a double sense. Where "everything is under control," the world no longer has anything to say to us, and where it has become newly uncontrollable, we can no longer hear it, because we cannot *reach* it.

Conclusion

This small book, and particularly its pessimistic conclusion, is certainly not definitive, and this is far from being the last word on the subject of where the boundary line between the controllable and the uncontrollable runs through modern society and how we should deal with the latter. It is only a first attempt to reflect on something that in my view constitutes the basic contradiction of modernity, a stopover on my journey of thinking about the relationship between resonance and control that I hope shines a new light on both our political problems and the personal problems of our daily lives, the internal and the external battles we wage every day. Perhaps it can also help with explaining where all the frustration and anger at modern life and society comes from, our despair over a world that nevertheless stands open to us and at our disposal in historically unprecedented ways. Our exasperation has its roots not in what is still denied to us, but in what we have lost because we now have it under our control.

Notes

Notes to Introduction

1 I owe this insight to Anton Röhr, who has written an impressive monograph on the ritual practices of tennis players titled "Ready? Play! Ein Versuch zum Zusammenhang von Ritual und Resonanz im Tennis" (Erfurt: Max Weber Kolleg, 2018).

Notes to Chapter 1

1 See Maurice Merleau-Ponty, *The Visible and the Invisible*, trans. by Alphonso Lingis (Evanston, IL: Northwestern University Press, 1968), 88.

2 See, for example, Max Scheler, *The Human Place in the Cosmos*, trans. by Manfred S. Frings (Evanston, IL: Northwestern University Press, 2009), as well as William James, *The Varieties of Religious Experience: A Study in Human Nature* (New York: Penguin, 1985).

3 See also Herbert Marcuse, *Eros and Civilization: A Philosophical Inquiry into Freud* (Boston: Beacon Press: 1974), 111 (quoting Max Scheler).

4 See Scheler, *The Human Place in the Cosmos* and Marcuse, *Eros and Civilization*. Marcuse meticulously describes how the "Promethean" principle of encountering the world with the aim of conquering it has evolved along with and been exacerbated by capitalist modernity, suppressing other possible ways of being in the world, particularly what he describes as an Orphean or erotic relationship to the world.

5 See Harmut Rosa, *Identität und kulturelle Praxis: Politische Philosophie nach Charles Taylor* (Frankfurt: Campus, 1998); Harmut Rosa, *Social Acceleration: A New Theory of Modernity*, trans. by Jonathan Trejo-Mathys (New York: Columbia University Press, 2013); and especially Harmut Rosa, *Resonance: A Sociology of Our Relationship to the World*, trans. by James C. Wagner (Cambridge: Polity, 2019).

6 See Rosa, *Resonance*, 309–310.

7 See Elisabeth von Thadden, *Die berührungslose Gesellschaft* (Munich: C. H. Beck, 2018).

Notes to Chapter 2

1 See Michaela Christ, "Die Zukunft liegt im Dunkeln: Dynamiken von Wachstum und künstlicher Beleuchtung in der Moderne," *psychosozial* 143.1 (2016): 11–24.

2 On the economic concept of the "land grab," see Klaus Dörre, "Landnahme: Triebkräfte, Wirkungen und Grenzen kapitalistischer Wachstumsdynamik," in Maria Backhouse, Olaf Gerlach, Stefan Kalmring, and Andreas Nowak, eds., *Die globale Einhegung: Krise, ursprüngliche Akkumulation*

und Landnahmen im Kapitalismus (Münster: Westfälisches Dampfboot, 2013), 112–141.

Notes to Chapter 3

1 For a critique of this conception of the environment, see Katharina Block's brilliant study *Von der Umwelt zur Welt: Die Bedeutung des Weltbegriffs für die Umweltsoziologie* (Koblenz: University of Koblenz-Landau, 2014).
2 Erhard Eppler and Niko Paech, *Was Sie da vorhaben, wäre ja eine Revolution: Ein Streitgespräch über Wachstum, Politik und eine Ethik des Genug, moderiert von Christiane Grefe* (Munich: Oekom-Verlag, 2016), 18–19.
3 Karl Marx, *Capital: A Critique of Political Economy*, vol. 1, trans. by Ben Fowkes (London: Penguin, 1990), 134.
4 "The relationship of the worker to labor engenders the relation to it of the capitalist [. . .]. *Private property* is thus the product, the result, the necessary consequence, of *alienated labor*, of the external relation of the work to nature and to himself. *Private property* thus results by analysis from the concept of *alienated labor*—i.e. of *alienated man*, of estranged labor, of estranged life, of *estranged* man." Marx, *Economic and Philosophic Manuscripts of 1844*, trans. by Martin Milligan (Mineola, NY: Dover, 1988), 80–81.
5 "Let us [. . .] clarify what this intellectual rationalization through science and scientific technology actually means in practice. Does it perhaps mean that today we [. . .] have a greater understanding of the conditions under which we live [. . .]? Hardly.

[. . .] It means something else—the knowledge or the belief that, if only one wanted to, one could find out any time; that there are in principle no mysterious, incalculable powers at work, but rather that one could in principle master everything through calculation. But that means the disenchantment of the world." Max Weber, "The Vocation of Science," in idem, *The Essential Weber: A Reader*, ed. by Sam Whimster (London: Routledge, 2004), 273–274. See also Max Weber, *Economy and Society: An Outline of Interpretive Sociology*, ed. by Guenther Roth and Claus Wittich (Berkeley: University of California Press, 1978); and Wolfgang Shuchter, *Die Entwicklung des okzidentalen Rationalismus: Eine Analyse von Max Webers Gesellschaftsgeschichte* (Tübingen: Mohr, 1979).

6 See Max Weber, *The Protestant Ethic and the "Spirit" of Capitalism and Other Writings*, ed. and trans. by Peter Baehr and Gordon C. Wells (New York: Penguin, 2002), 121, and Hartmut Rosa, *Resonance: A Sociology of Our Relationship to the World*, trans. by James C. Wagner (Cambridge: Polity, 2019), 325–329.

7 Georg Simmel, "The Metropolis and Modern Life," in idem, *Simmel on Culture: Selected Writings*, ed. by David Frisby and Mike Featherstone (London: SAGE, 1997), 174–186, here 179.

8 Ibid., 178.

9 See Friedrich Schiller, "The Gods of Greece," in idem, *Works of Friedrich Schiller*, vol. 1.2, ed. by Nathan Haskell Dole (Boston, MA: C. T. Brainard, 1902), 156–160 (for all the quotations in this paragraph).

10 Among contemporary authors, Michel Houellebecq describes a similar world in his novel *Atomised* (London: Vintage Books, 2001), the title of which alone already suggests relationlessness.

11 Albert Camus, "The Myth of Sisyphus," in idem, *The Myth of Sisyphus and Other Essays*, trans. by Justin O'Brien (New York: Vintage International, 1991), 14.

12 Ibid., 21.

13 See Hannah Arendt, *The Human Condition* (Chicago, IL: University of Chicago Press, 1958); and Hannah Arendt, "Kultur und Politik," in eadem, ed., *Zwischen Vergangenheit und Zukunft: Übungen im politischen Denken* (Munich: Piper, 1958), 277–302. On Arendt's concept of the world, see also Uta-D. Rose, "Lebenswelt und politische Welt: Ein phänomenologische Analyse," a lecture delivered as part of the 21st Convention of the German Society for Philosophy, September 15–19, 2008, http://www.dgphil2008.de/fileadmin/download/Sektionsbeitraege/14-3_Rose and Paul Sörensen, *Entfremdung als Schlüsselbegriff einer kritischen Theorie der Politik: Ein Systematisierungsversuch im Ausgang von Hannah Arendt und Cornelius Castoriadis* (Jena: University of Jena, 2014).

14 See Harmut Rosa, *Resonance: A Sociology of Our Relationship to the World*, trans. by James C. Wagner (Cambridge: Polity, 2019), 305–377. On burnout as a cultural phenomenon, see also Alain Ehrenberg, *The Weariness of the Self: Diagnosing the History of Depression in the Contemporary Age*, trans. by Enrico Caouette et al. (Montreal: McGill-Queen's University Press, 2010) and Sighard Neckel and Greta Wagner,

"Erschöpfung als 'schöpferische Zerstörung': Burnout und gesellschaftlicher Wandel," in Sighard Neckel and Greta Wagner, eds., *Leistung und Erschöpfung: Burnout in der Wettbewerbsgesellschaft* (Berlin: Suhrkamp, 2013), 203–218.

Notes to Chapter 4

1 Eccentric positionality is a concept developed by Helmuth Plessner in his *Levels of Organic Life and the Human: An Introduction to Philosophical Anthropology*, trans. by Milllay Hyatt (New York: Fordham University Press, 2019). See also Max Scheler, *The Human Place in the Cosmos*, trans. by Manfred S. Frings (Evanston, IL: Northwestern University Press, 2009).

2 Maurice Merleau-Ponty, "The Metaphysical in Man," in idem, *Sense and NonSense*, trans. by Hubert L. Drefyus and Patricia Allen Drefyus (Evanston, IL: Northwestern University Press, 1964), 83–98, here 94. See Bernhard Waldenfels, *Antwortregister* (Frankfurt am Main: Suhrkamp, 2007) and Lambert Wiesing, *Das Mich der Wahrnehmung: Eine Autopsie* (Frankfurt am Main: Suhrkamp, 2009).

3 See Brian Massumi, *Parables for the Virtual: Movement, Affect, Sensation* (Durham, NC: Duke University Press, 2002).

4 This view also seems to contradict not only *poetic* experience, but also our *everyday* experience, in which things and materials "address" us or "appeal" to us, or "leave us cold," in a variety of ways. See Hartmut Rosa, *Resonance: A Sociology of Our Relationship to the World*, trans. James C. Wagner (Cambridge: Polity, 2019), 226–257.

Notes to Chapter 5

1 On the categorial difference between resonance and echo, see Hartmut Rosa, *Resonance: A Sociology of Our Relationship to the World*, trans. James C. Wagner (Cambridge: Polity, 2019), 182–183, 191, 219–220.

2 See Hartmut Rosa, "Heimat als anverwandelter Weltausschnitt: Ein resonanztheoretischer Verusch," in Edoardo Costadura, Klaus Ries, and Christiane Wiesenfeld, eds., *Heimat global: Modelle, Praxen und Medien der Heimatkonstruktion* (Bielefeld: transcript, 2019), 153–172; Hartmut Rosa, "Heimat im Zeitalter der Globalisierung," *Der Blaue Reiter: Journal für Philosophie* 23 (2007): 19–23.

3 Igor Levit, "Es ist so unheimlich geil," *Die Zeit*, May 19, 2016. https://www.zeit.de/2016/22/igor-levit-pianist-jubilaeum-ludwig-van-beethoven-klaviersonaten.

4 "[T]he word *will*, which is supposed to unlock the innermost essence of all things in nature for us like a magic spell [. . .] does not have the slightest connotation of an unknown quantity or the result of an inference; rather, it refers to something of which we have immediate cognition, something so thoroughly familiar that we know and understand what will is much better than anything else, whatever it may be. —Until now people have subsumed the concept of *will* under the concept of *force*. I will do precisely the opposite, and let every force in nature be known as will. Do not think this is just a quibble over terms or a matter of indifference: it is in fact a matter of the greatest significance and importance." Arthur Schopenhauer, *The World as Will and Representation*,

ed. and trans. by Judith Norman, Alistair Welchman, and Christopher Janaway (Cambridge: Cambridge University Press, 2010), vol. 1, 136.

5 Charles Taylor, "Resonanz und die Romantik," in Christian Helge Peters and Peter Schulz, eds., *Resonanzen udn Dissonanzen: Hartmut Rosas kiritsche Theorie in der Diskussion* (Bielefeld: transcript, 2017), 249–270.

6 For a physio-theoretical approach in the mold of new materialism, see Karen Barad, "Meeting the Universe Halfway: Realism and Social Constructivism without Contradiction," in Lynn Hankinson and Jack Nelson, eds., *Feminism, Science, and the Philosophy of Science* (Dordrecht: Kluver, 1996), 161–194. For an attempt at a "symmetrical anthropology" that conceives of things, like people, as actors or actants, see Bruno Latour, *We Have Never Been Modern*, trans. Catherine Porter (Cambridge, MA: Harvard University Press, 1993).

7 Erich Fromm, *To Have or to Be?* (London: Bloomsbury Academic, 2013).

8 See Anna Höcker, Margarita Engberding, and Fred Rist, *Prokrastination: Ein Manual zur Behandlung des pathologischen Aufschiebens* (Göttingen: Hogrefe, 2017).

9 See Albert Bandura, "Perceived Self-Efficacy in Cognitive Development and Functioning," *Educational Psychologist* 28 (1993): 117–148.

10 Mihaly Csikszentmihalyi, *Flow: The Psychology of Optimal Experience* (New York: HarperCollins, 1991). See also Thomas Schmaus, *Philosophie des Flow-Erlebens: Ein Zugang zum Denken Heinrich Rombachs* (Stuttgart: Kohlhammer, 2012).

11 The term "partial controllability" might at first glance seem more incisive, or at least more professional, but upon closer inspection proves to be incorrect. We are dealing here not with identifiable individual parts that are either controllable or uncontrollable, but with a relationship that, although it cannot be controlled in its entirety, can very well be influenced. "Semicontrollability" thus points to the difference between controllability and reachability.

12 See Martin Pfleiderer and Hartmut Rosa, "Musik als Resonanzsphäre," *Musik & Ästhetik* 24.95 (2020), forthcoming.

13 It would be extremely interesting to attempt to elaborate in this way a sociology of sport based on resonance theory. This might very well explain why soccer is more popular than handball worldwide, for example. Meanwhile, secure control of the ball with one's hands does not detract from the popularity of basketball, because the *basket* provides the aspect of uncontrollability.

14 Hermann Deuser, "Unverfügbarkeit," in Rolf Gröschner, Antje Kapust, and Oliver Lembcke, eds., *Wörterbuch der Würde* (Munich: Wilhelm Fink, 2013), 202–203. See also Rudolf Bultmann, *Theologische Enzyklopädie*, ed. by Eberhard Jüngel and Klaus W. Müller (Tübingen: Mohr Siebeck, 1984). On the history of the term, see Hans Vorster, "Unverfügbarkeit," in Joachim Ritter and Karlfried Gründer, eds., *Historisches Wörterbuch der Philosophie*, vol. 11 (Darmstadt: Wissenschaftliche Buchgesellschaft, 2001), 331–336.

15 For a number of interesting reflections on and critiques of the concept of resonance, see Tobias Kläden

and Michael Schüßler, eds., *Zu schnell für Gott? Theologische Kontroversen zu Beschleunigung und Resonanz* (Freiburg: Herder, 2017).

16 See Deuser, "Unverfügbarkeit," 203.

Notes to Chapter 6

1 For a number of highly illuminating reflections and positions on this and all other aspects of the relationship between medical feasibility and fate, from birth to death, see Giovanni Maio, ed., *Abschaffung des Schicksals? Menschen zwischen Gegebenheit des Lebens und medizing-technischer Gestaltbarkeit* (Freiburg: Herder, 2014).

2 See Franziska Rupp, "Subjektive Erfahrung der Geburt von Müttern in Wet- und Ost-Berlin vor (1950–1989) und nach (1990–2015) der Wiedervereinigung," *Refubium: Repositorium der FU Berlin*, September 13, 2018. https://refubium.fu-berlin.de/handle/fub188/22848.

3 See Leon Hempel, Susanne Krasmann, and Ulrich Bröckling, eds., *Sichtbarkeitsregime: Überwachung, Sicherheit und Privatheit im 21. Jahrhundert* (Wiesbaden: Springer VS, 2010).

4 Hence it should come as no surprise that children and adolescents themselves exhibit low expectations of self-efficacy, and thus an incapacity for resonance, when it comes to dealing with their own bodies. As a longtime educator with the Deutsche SchülerAkademie, an extracurricular program for gifted high school students in Germany, I have noticed that the number of adolescents who demand medical attention even for the most minor physical ailments seems to keep rising year after year.

5 See Rudolf Tippelt, ed., *Steuerung durch Indikatoren: Methodologische und theoretische Reflektionen zur deutschen und internationalen Bildungsberichterstattung* (Leverkusen: Barbara Budrich, 2009); Mustafa Yunus Eryaman and Barbara Schneider, eds., *Evidence and Public Good in Educational Policy, Research, and Practice* (Cham: Springer International Publishing, 2017).

6 See Hartmut Rosa, *Resonance: A Sociology of Our Relationship to the World*, trans. James C. Wagner (Cambridge: Polity, 2019), 238–248; Hartmut Rosa and Wolfgang Endres, *Resonanzpädagogik* (Weinheim: Beltz, 2017).

7 At the University of Jena, for example, an Institut für Bildung und Kultur (Institute for Education and Culture) split off from the Institut für Erziehungswissenschaft (Institute for Educational Science).

8 Rico Nil et al., "Burnout: Eine Standortbestimmung," *Schweizer Archiv dür Neurologie und Psychiatrie* 161.2 (2010): 72–77.

9 This is a quotation from a highly talented, eighteen-year-old graduate of the Deutsche SchülerAkademie, where, much to my amazement, such sentiments are commonly heard among the adolescent participants year after year. [NB 'literal' is in the definition of 'quotation' (if it's not literal it's paraphrase or something else]

10 Woody Allen, "The Lunatic's Tale," in idem, *Side Effects* (New York: Ballantine Books, 1980), 99–110.

11 Elisabeth von Thadden, *Die berührungslose Gesellschaft* (Munich: C. H. Beck, 2018), n.p.

12 Julia Schreiber has shown that physical exercise involves a shift in our attention from being a phenomenal body, which is fundamentally uncontrollable, to having a physical body. See Julia Schneider, *Körperpraxis und Leiberleben im Kontext spätmoderner Optimierungsanforderungen*, PhD dissertation (Goethe University Frankfurt, 2018).

13 Giovanni Maio, "Gefangen im Übermaß an Ansprüchen und Verheißungen: Zur Bedeutung des Schicksals für das Denken der modernen Medizin," in idem, ed., *Abschaffung des Schicksals* (Freiburg: Herder, 2016), 10–48, here 35.

14 Ibid., 34–35.

15 Alfons Maurer, "Das Resonanzkonzept und die Altenhilfe: Zum Einsatz digitaler Technik in der Pflege," in Jean-Pierre Wils, ed., *Resonanz: Im interdisziplinären Gespräch mit Hartmut Rosa* (Baden-Baden: Nomos, 2019).

16 Maio, "Gefangen im Übermaß," 31.

Notes to Chapter 7

1 Those not satisfied with news reports can find well-elaborated theoretical arguments for this in Niklas Luhmann's systems theory as well as in Ulrich Beck's theory of reflexive modernization. The former argues that politics, like every other social sphere (economy, science, education, etc.), functions "autopoietically," that is, according to its own standards, "codes," and perspectives, and thus cannot exert control over other areas but at most only irritate them. The latter demonstrates that the side effects of political (and technological) action always outweigh the intended effects. See Niklas

Luhmann, *Political Theory in the Welfare State*, trans. John Bednarz (Berlin: de Gruyter, 1990); Ulrich Beck, Anthony Giddens, and Scott Lash, *Reflexive Modernization: Politics, Tradition and Aesthetics in the Modern Social Order* (Cambridge: Polity, 1994).

2 Max Weber, *Economy and Society: An Outline of Interpretive Sociology*, ed. by Guenther Roth and Claus Wittich (Berkeley: University of California Press, 1978), 217–223, 956–1002.

3 See Tilo Wesche, "Der Wert des Eigentums: Über die Propriation der Zeit," in *WestEnd: Neue Zeitschrift für Sozialforschung* 1 (2018): 129–142.

4 For Helmuth Plessner, see Katharina Block, *Von der Umwelt zur Welt: Die Bedeutung des Weltbegriffs für die Umweltsoziologie* (Koblenz: University of Koblenz-Landau, 2014).

5 Theodor W. Adorno, *Negative Dialectics*, trans. E. B. Ashton (New York: Continuum, 1973).

6 Rainer Maria Rilke, "I Am So Afraid of People's Words," in idem, *Selected Poems with Parallel German Text*, ed. by Robert Vilain, trans. by Susan Ranson and Marielle Sutherland (Oxford: Oxford University Press, 2011), 7.

7 The works of the internationally renowned quantum physicist Anton Zeilinger are highly instructive in this context. See Anton Zeilinger, *Einsteins Spuk: Teleportation und weitere Mysterien der Quantenphysik* (Munich: Goldmann, 2007).

Notes to Chapter 8

1 Harry Frankfurt, "Freedom of the Will and the Concept of a Person," *Journal of Philosophy* 68 (1971): 5–20.

2 On the concept of "strong evaluations," see Charles Taylor, "What Is Human Agency?" in idem, *Human Agency and Language: Philosophical Papers* 1 (Cambridge: Cambridge University Press, 1985), 15–44. See Hartmut Rosa, *Identität und kulturelle Praxis: Politische Philosophie nach Charles Taylor* (Frankfurt: Campus, 1998), 98–126.

3 This is a modified version of "commodity fetishism," as elaborated by Karl Marx in the first chapter of the first volume of *Capital*.

4 See Albert O. Hirschman, *A Propensity to Self-Subversion* (Cambridge, MA: Harvard University Press, 1996).

5 Irene Berkel, ed., *Postsexualität: Zur Transformation des Begehrens* (Gießen: Psychosozial-Verlag, 2009); Peter Kuemmel, "Jeder mit jedem: Aus dem postsexuellen Zeitalter: Thomas Ostermeier inszeniert Biljana Srbljanovics 'Supermarkt' in Wien," *Die Zeit*, June 21, 2001.

6 See Hartmut Rosa, *Resonance: A Sociology of Our Relationship to the World*, trans. by James C. Wagner (Cambridge: Polity, 2019), 110–144.

Notes to Chapter 9

1 In my view, the most interesting book on this subject remains John Urry, *Global Complexity* (Cambridge: Polity, 2003).

2 Robert J. Oppenheimer, "The New Weapon: The Turn of the Screw," in Dexter Masters and

Katharine Way, eds., *One World or None: A Report to the Public on the Full Meaning of the Atomic Bomb* (New York: New Press, 2007), 58–61.

3 On the idea that the spirit of modernity has given birth to monsters, see Bruno Latour, *We Have Never Been Modern*, trans. by Catherine Porter (Cambridge, MA: Harvard University Press, 1993).